KEYSTONES *for* READING

COMPREHENSION ▪ VOCABULARY ▪ STUDY SKILLS

Level D

Alden J. Moe, Ph.D.
Lehigh University

Sandra S. Dahl, Ph.D.
University of Wisconsin

Carol J. Hopkins, Ph.D.
Purdue University

John W. Miller, Ph.D.
Georgia Southern College

Elayne Ackerman Moe, M.Ed.
Educational Consultant

MODERN CURRICULUM PRESS

Table of Contents

A People Count

When you were born, one more person was added to the population of your city. In this lesson, you will read about how people are counted. You will learn special words about places and where people live.

 ## 1 KEYS to Content Words

Every subject has special content words.

LEARN Every subject has its own special words. We call these words *content words*. Content words help you get the most meaning from what you read.

DIRECTIONS Use the content words to help you answer the questions.

resident: person who lives in a particular area
continent: large mass of land

Continent	Population
Asia	2,760,000,000
Europe	695,000,000
Africa	520,000,000
North America	390,000,000
South America	260,000,000
Australia	16,000,000
Antarctica	0

NEW CARLISLE
POP. 6,498

1. Which continent has the most residents? __Asia__

2. How many residents does your continent have?
   __390,000,000__

2 Practice With Content Words

DIRECTIONS Read the article. Match each content word from the list with its definition. Write each word on the correct line.

In many countries, people are counted every ten years. This official count is called a census. Census takers go to residents' homes to get information. Census figures are used to find the size of the population. The census also gives us other information like age, sex, education, and occupation of the people.

In some countries, there has not been a census for many years. In other countries, the people have never been counted. Therefore, we can only estimate, or guess, the number of people living in these places.

The number of people who live in a specified area is called its population. Census figures tell us Asia has over half the world's population, while Antarctica has a population of zero. The climate of Antarctica is so cold that only a few scientists live there for part of the year.

census taker   population
estimate   census
climate   continents

1. a population count:

   Census

2. the seven main land masses:

   Continents

3. person who gathers census information:

   Official

4. used where a census cannot be taken:

   estimate

5. number of residents in a specific area:

   Population

6. weather conditions:

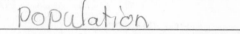
   Climate

Read and Apply

Some parts of every continent have very few people. In some places, it is cold most of the year. Few people live in very cold places because it is too cold for most plants to grow. The largest areas of cold land are very far north or very far south. The northern parts of North America, Europe and Asia are cold much of the year. The southernmost continent, Antarctica, is the coldest region of the world.

There are very few people in the world's large deserts. Since deserts get so little rain, it is difficult to grow crops. Deserts cover almost one-fourth of the world's land surface. The largest desert is in northern Africa, but North America, Asia, and Australia also have deserts.

Some other parts of the world with very few people are the hot and wet areas near the Equator. The hot, wet climates produce jungles. There are areas of South America, Africa, and Asia with so much rain that living is very difficult. One example is the land along the Amazon River in South America. Another jungle is near the Congo River in Africa.

1. Which four continents have deserts? _Africa ✓_
   North America ✓   _Asia ✓_   _Australia ✓_

2. Which three continents have jungles? _South America_
   Africa   _Asia_

3. Name three kinds of places where the population is low.
   cold places   _hot places_   _Jungles._

DIRECTIONS The outline map of the world shows the seven continents and the four oceans. The line through the map is the Equator. Use the map and the articles you read in this lesson to help you answer the questions.

1. Mark a D on the continents on the map where deserts are found.

2. Mark a J on the continents where jungles are found.

3. Write "Brrrr" on the coldest continent on the map.

4. The continent of _Africa_ is almost cut in half by the Equator.

5. The continents of _Asia_ and _Europe_ together form a large area called Eurasia.

6. The _ATLantic_ Ocean separates North America and Europe.

7. The continents that lie completely north of the Equator are _North America_, _Asia_, and _Africa_.

8. The _Pacific_ ocean separates Asia and North America.

9. The continents that lie totally south of the Equator are _Atlantic_ and _____.

10. The _INDIAIV_ Ocean is east of North America, while the _Pacific_ Ocean is on the western border.

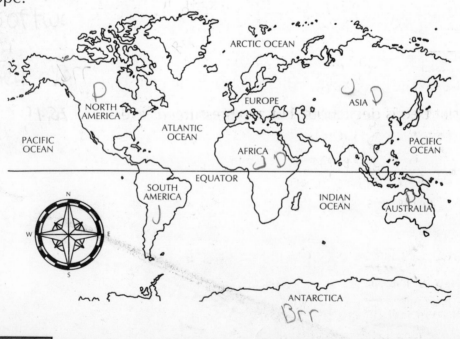

REMEMBER Special words help you get the most from your reading.

A Tree's Clothing

The wonder of trees is often the subject of poems. In this lesson, you'll learn some special words as you read about trees.

1   KEYS to Content Words

There are special words for every subject area.

LEARN   Content words are special words about a specific topic. Understanding the meaning of content words helps you learn more about special topics.

EXAMPLE   A chestnut tree is deciduous, but a cypress tree is evergreen.

The sentence is meaningful when you know that *deciduous* trees lose their leaves and later grow new leaves, while *evergreens* keep their green color all year by growing new leaves before shedding their old ones.

DIRECTIONS Read the paragraph. Then read each question and circle all correct answers.

    A chestnut tree is deciduous, but a cypress tree is evergreen. Deciduous trees, such as the birch, beech, ash, and maple, are valued by landscapers for their autumn leaf colors and for the fruits or berries they produce. Some evergreen trees, such as pines, firs, spruces, and hemlocks, have needles and bear cones.

1. Which trees would be bare during part of the year?
   hemlock   (maple)   cypress   (chestnut)   (birch)

2. Which trees provide greenery all year?
   (pine)   (hemlock)   beech   (spruce)   (fir)

Content Words **5**

DIRECTIONS Read each word and its meaning. Then use each word once as you complete the sentences below.

conifer—an evergreen tree that bears cones
broadleaf—a tree with broad, flat leaves
hardwood—a broadleaf tree, usually deciduous
softwood—a conifer
botanist—one who studies trees
needleleaf—a tree with needles, usually evergreen
sapling—a young tree that is 6 feet or more in height
seedling—a small tree grown from a seed

1. A _botanist_ would identify the red mulberry and black locust as deciduous trees.

2. A full-grown spruce, an evergreen that bears cones and has needles, could be called a _conifer_, _needleleaf_, or a _softwood_.

3. A seven-foot tree with a trunk from 1 to 2 inches thick is called a _sapling_.

4. Since the holly tree keeps its broad leaves all year, it is one of the few _broad leaf_ trees that is classified as an evergreen.

5. A baby tree barely beginning life is called a _seedling_.

6. An oak or maple table would be made from a _hardwood_ tree that loses its broad leaves in autumn.

Read and Apply

Read about seasonal changes in some trees, and how this occurence is observed by a poet.

A young leaf begins as a small bump, or bud, on a branch. The bud contains tiny leaves which are tightly packed together. A bud is important to the tree as the beginning of new leaves and also as a protective covering to the stem. Buds help a stem keep its moisture and offer protection from animals, insects, and harsh weather conditions.

The bud opens when the warm days and spring rains come. As the new light green leaves unfold, they take their food from older leaves or from the tree's stored food supply. As leaves mature, they turn a deeper green color and begin to produce food.

Although leaves provide food for animals and release oxygen into the air so other living things can breathe, their main job is to make food for the tree. Leaves make food by a process called photosynthesis, using light from the sun, carbon dioxide from the air, and water. Water is absorbed from the earth by a tree's roots. It is carried to the leaves through the sapwood, a layer of wood beneath the bark. Water is carried onward through the stems and into the veins of the leaves.

A leaf's green color comes from a substance, or pigment, called chlorophyll. There is so much chlorophyll in the leaves that it hides the red and yellow colors that are also in most leaves. In autumn, however, the chlorophyll breaks down in the leaves of deciduous trees. This is when leaves show their other colors, which may include purples and scarlets.

As the coolness of winter approaches, the stems clog and water is no longer passed to the leaves. Without water and an abundance of chlorophyll, the leaves of deciduous trees can no longer make food. The leaves become dry, turn brown, and eventually fall to the ground.

Silly Trees

I'm glad I'm me, and not a tree!
Some trees and I, we don't agree
On how to dress and what to wear
Upon our limbs and in our hair.
In summertime, when it is hot,
These trees wear all the clothes they've got!
And then in winter, when there's ice and snow,
They stand there nude from head to toe!
You'd think they'd learn from year to year
To wear their clothes in weather severe!
Not me! Oh, no! You'll not find me
Standing nude in winter like a silly old tree!

—Babs Bell Hajdusiewicz

DIRECTIONS Use the article and poem as you answer the questions.

1. What are three purposes of leaves? Leaves make food for animals, they also make oxygen   Leaves make food by process photosyn

2. What passes water from a tree's roots to its leaves? It passes into the stem

3. What substance causes a leaf's green color? Chlorophyll

4. What kind of trees are the topic of the poem? Silly trees

5. How do leaves begin? it begins as a small bump or bud Also on a branc

6. What is a leaf's food-making process called? It is called photosynthesis

7. What are leaves compared to in the poem? They don't have leaves.

REMEMBER Special words are unique to each subject.

Finding the Prize

Do you like to solve puzzles? Do you ever get frustrated while trying to solve a problem? In this lesson, you will read about two boys who had to solve a frustrating puzzle to get something they wanted. You will learn about words that have the same meaning.

1 KEYS to Synonyms

Synonyms share the same meaning.

LEARN A synonym is a word that means nearly the same thing as another word. Synonyms can help you say the same thing in a different way.

EXAMPLE The boys had to solve a puzzle.
The boys had to solve a problem.

Puzzle and *problem* are synonyms because both words tell what the boys had to solve.

DIRECTIONS Find a word from the list that means the same thing or nearly the same thing as each underlined word. Write the synonym on the line.

locate   ~~father~~   ~~hint~~   ~~start~~   ~~fool~~

1. Please give us just one <u>clue</u>. _____ *hint* ✓

2. How will we <u>find</u> the prize? _____ *locate* ✓

3. The boys must <u>begin</u> looking. _____ *start* ✓

4. Their <u>dad</u> gave them a hard puzzle. _____ *father* ✓

5. Was he trying to <u>trick</u> the boys? _____ *fool* ✓

2 Practice With Synonyms

DIRECTIONS Read the story. Find each numbered word in the story, and circle it. Find the correct synonym in the list on the right. Write it on the line. Does the sentence mean the same thing with either word?

Tyrone and Jesse needed baseball gloves, and they needed them right away. Baseball practice would begin tomorrow. Their coach would not permit anyone to play without a mitt.

The boys knew Dad had bought their mitts. They knew they were hidden somewhere in the house. Dad enjoyed giving his sons "little problems" to solve. He called the problems "brain teasers."

"This is not funny!" wailed Jesse. "We have to have those mitts. If we miss practice, we can't be on the team."

"Please, Dad, give us a clue," the boys whined.

Dad lowered his newpaper. "All right, just one clue. A pentagon is the shape of an object in our house."

"What kind of clue is that?" moaned Jesse.

1. funny _____amusing_____ (mitts)

2. hidden _____concealed_____ liked

3. object _____thing_____ (purchased)

4. bought _____purchased_____ (type)

5. permit _____allow_____ (concealed)

6. gloves _____mitts_____ (amusing)

7. enjoyed _____liked_____ (allow)

8. kind _____type_____ (thing)

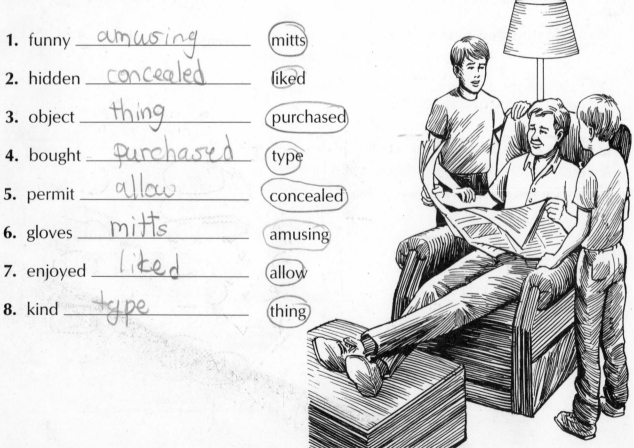

3 Read and Apply

DIRECTIONS Read more of the story. Find a group of words in the story that is almost like each numbered group of words. Write the synonym from the story for each underlined word.

Tyrone and Jesse thought and thought. Suddenly Jesse yelled, "I'll bet I know where those baseball gloves are!"

He ran out to the garage with Tyrone rushing breathlessly after him. There, hanging above a trash can, was a poster that looked like a stop sign. Tyrone helped Jesse tug at the lid. The boys peered in and the corners of their mouths turned down. There was nothing in the can.

The garage door was opening. Somehow the boys knew who was there.

"That stop sign has eight angles and eight sides. An octagon is not a pentagon, fellas," said Dad.

Tyrone suddenly remembered a strange-looking box he'd noticed in the hall closet. He beckoned to his brother. Tyrone pulled a hatbox from the shelf. Inside the box were winter hats and nothing else. The boys saw Dad's face peering around the corner.

"Sorry, guys. That box has six angles and six sides. A hexagon is certainly not a pentagon. Keep thinking!"

1. Tyrone running breathlessly after him

   rushing ✓

2. A hexagon is surely not a pentagon.

   certainly ✓

3. Dad's face looking around the corner

   peering ✓

4. helped Jesse pull at the lid

   tug ✓

5. he'd seen in the hall closet

   notice ✓

6. hanging above a garbage can

   thrash ✓

Tyrone and Jesse slumped down on the stairs. They didn't want to think. They wanted to play baseball. Dad's game was too hard. They would never find the mitts in time.

"I know!" said Jesse. "Let's look up *pentagon* in the dictionary."

When they looked up *pentagon,* this is what they found:

pentagon (pen' tə gon): a plane figure having five sides and five angles.

"I think I know," Tyrone whispered to Jesse. "Remember that old home plate in the basement?"

"I sure do," answered Jesse. "That must be a pentagon. Let's go!"

The boys ran to the basement. They searched and searched until they found the home plate. Under the home plate in a pile of sports equipment, they found two brand-new baseball gloves.

Tyrone and Jesse grinned at each other.

"We did it!" they yelled. "We solved the problem."

Tyrone and Jesse raced up the stairs and out the door. They couldn't wait to try out their new mitts. They hadn't noticed their Dad grinning in a dark corner of the basement.

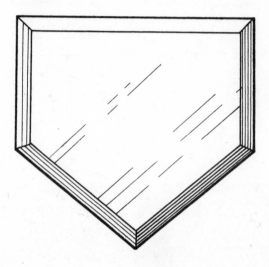

DIRECTIONS Circle the two words in each row that are synonyms.

1. walked   (ran)   jumped   (raced)
2. (difficult)   easy   (hard)   different
3. (unused)   old   dark   (new)
4. (smiling)   (grinning)   frowning   wondering
5. bold   (dim)   (dark)   lighted
6. hunted   (discovered)   (found)   saved
7. (cellar)   attic   (basement)   closed
8. (wondered)   (wanted)   wished   found
9. (figure)   word   blank   (shape)
10. around   (under)   over   (beneath)

REMEMBER Synonyms mean the same, or almost the same, thing.

A Mountain or a Molehill?

Did you ever worry too much about something? In this lesson, you'll read about a girl who tries to learn to relax. You'll also learn about words that have opposite meanings.

1 KEYS to Antonyms

Antonyms are words whose meanings are opposites.

LEARN Using an antonym for one or two words in a sentence changes the meaning of the whole sentence.

EXAMPLE The failure was partly his.
The success was entirely his.

The sentences have different meanings because of the antonyms.

DIRECTIONS Match the words in the word box with their antonyms below. Write the word on the line.

~~wonderful~~	~~allowed~~	agreement	~~indirectly~~
~~curved~~	~~borrowed~~	~~northern~~	selfish
~~grouchy~~	exhausted	~~dangerously~~	~~rude~~

1. forbidden ___allowed ✓___
2. safely ___dangerously ✓___
3. straight ___curved ✓___
4. directly ___indirectly ✓___

5. pleasant ___grouchy ✓___
6. repaid ___borrowed ✓___
7. generous ___selfish ✓___
8. southern ___northen ✓___

2 Practice With Antonyms

DIRECTIONS Read each sentence. Circle the antonym for the underlined word.

1. Frankie <u>refused</u> the money for mowing the grass.

   dismissed   objected   (accepted)   answered

2. We are <u>content</u> with the way things are going.

   (satisfied)   comfortable   hopeful   dissatisfied

3. There are <u>numerous</u> choices to be made.

   many   general   (few)   different

4. The group <u>donated</u> the profits from the fund-raiser.

   received   (denied)   corrected   renewed

5. Janice <u>omitted</u> the last three problems.

   released   forgot   (included)   (permitted)

6. The rules stated a <u>maximum</u> of two entries.

   limitation   (minimum)   majority   ruling

7. The <u>ugliness</u> of the landscape went unnoticed.

   misuse   view   (beauty)   abuse

8. I appreciated the action of my <u>opponent</u>.

   (teammate)   enemy   rival   coach

9. This exercise is somewhat <u>risky</u>.

   dangerous   (harmless)   threatening   difficult

10. We were excited at <u>dismissal</u> time.

   departure   closing   finishing   (arrival)

11. I <u>doubt</u> that you are really going to do it.

   (believe)   hope   promise   question

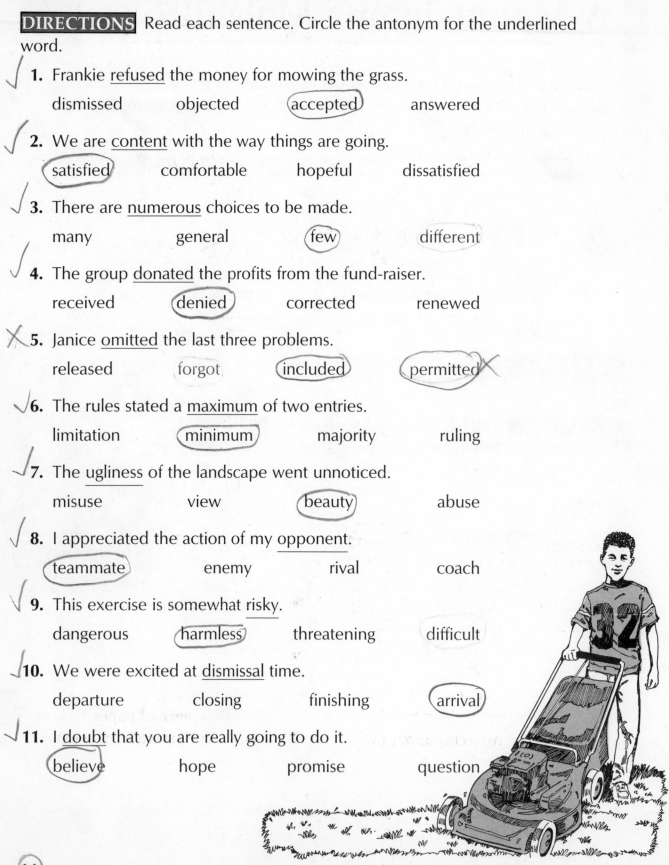

3 Read and Apply

DIRECTIONS Read about learning to control unnecessary worrying.

Peggy knew she tended to be a "worry-wart." Her mom was always saying that Peggy made mountains out of molehills. She couldn't help it, though. There were just so many things to worry about. What if her cat got sick? What if her tennis match on Saturday had to be cancelled because of rain?

Today, Peggy had more than her share of worries on top of the usual ones. Mr. Dibbs had just announced that some special tests were to begin next week. He told the class that the tests were to see how much they had learned all year. He said they could not study for this kind of test. He said that the tests would not affect their grades. The only thing they needed to do to prepare was to get a good night's sleep and eat a good breakfast before coming to school each day.

In spite of his efforts, Mr. Dibbs could see that Peggy was worried. He tried to tell her that she should relax. She was a good student and did well on tests. Nothing seemed to work. He noticed the serious frown on Peggy's face. He decided to think of a way to help her relax about the tests. He thought he had a plan.

The next day, Mr. Dibbs gave a surprise quiz in social studies to begin his plan. Before the test, he told his students to look at their papers and repeat what he said exactly as he said it.

"You are a piece of paper," Mr. Dibbs said, and his students repeated his sentence.

"You are simply a piece of paper with words," he went on. Peggy and her classmates repeated what he'd said.

"I am an intelligent person," Mr. Dibbs continued, pausing only for the students to repeat. "You are a silly old piece of paper . . . but I am a clever human being. . . . A silly piece of paper is no match for my brain. . . . You are a flat, boring piece of paper . . . but I am a smart human being. . . . No way will I let a piece of paper . . . worry smart, intelligent me. . . ."

Peggy was smiling. She looked up at Mr. Dibbs who had already noticed she was no longer frowning. "Hey, Mr. Dibbs! Maybe this silly talk will help me on those tests next week! I'll have to think about that."

DIRECTIONS Match each numbered word with its antonym from the list at the right. Write the antonym on the line.

1. continuing	_____	frowning
2. regular	_____	worried
3. forgotten	_____	pausing
4. ignored	_____	beginning
5. carefree	_____	remembered
6. smiling	_____	noticed
7. ending	_____	special
8. healthy	_____	molehills
9. after	_____	common
10. unusual	_____	intelligent
11. dull	_____	tense
12. funny	_____	sick
13. relaxed	_____	before
14. mountains	_____	serious

REMEMBER An antonym changes the whole meaning of a sentence.

A Useful Trick

Sometimes a trick can become more than a joke. In this lesson, you'll learn about words that sound the same as you read about two boys whose tricks proved to be useful.

 ## 1 KEYS to Homonyms

Homonyms are words that sound alike but have different spellings.

LEARN There are many pairs of words that sound alike but are spelled differently and have different meanings. The words around a homonym help you know which word to use.

DIRECTIONS Write one word from each homonym pair on the line.

1. The owner of the house showed us the storage room in the _____.
   seller—one who sells something
   cellar—a basement used for storage

2. This belt barely fits around my _____.
   waist—part of the body around the middle
   waste—to damage or throw away

3. His _____ for food were not answered.
   please—a polite word used when asking
           for something
   pleas—requests for help in some way

4. Mom asked for some _____ and quiet.
   piece—part of something
   peace—without war, calm

Homonyms **17**

Practice With Homonyms

DIRECTIONS Read each pair of sentences and circle the homonyms. Then write the correct homonym on the line before each meaning below.

1. We walked out on the pier at dusk.

2. I saw him peer in the window.

   _____ : look closely

   _____ : structure extending into the water

3. Have you seen the high school play?

4. The last scene is especially good.

   _____ : part of a play or production

   _____ : noticed or viewed

5. The cowboys gave a whoop as they rode off.

6. Mom uses a hoop to hold her needlework fabric.

   _____ : a loud shout

   _____ : a frame in the shape of a circle or oval

7. It will lessen your work load if I help you.

8. I have a piano lesson at noon tomorrow.

   _____ : learning with a teacher

   _____ : to make smaller

9. The thumb tacks are missing from the bulletin board.

10. This notebook cost $1.98 plus tax.

    _____ : money paid to run the government

    _____ : small pointed nails

DIRECTIONS Look for words that have homonyms as you read about a back-up plan that fooled an audience.

Ron and Rich were fraternal twins. They looked quite different. They never wore matching clothes. They were twins-in-disguise until they opened their mouths. Their voices sounded exactly alike. The boys enjoyed playing tricks on people, but little did they dream that their trickery might come in handy someday.

Early each school year, their favorite trick, talking for each other, would cause quite a scene. If the teacher asked Ron a question, he would sit silently and stare at the teacher while Rich answered from another part of the room.

Once, however, the boys' trick was a huge help. Preparations for their class play were nearly done. The big day was near when they would present it for their parents and the whole school. Ron had the lead part and Rich had worked on one of the crews backstage.

Just one day before the play, Ron became hoarse. Everyone was upset at the thought of postponing the production until Ron could talk again. Just when it seemed they would have to postpone the play, Rich had an idea. Ron could move his mouth on stage as if saying his lines and he, Rich, could read the script from the side of the stage out of sight!

Their teacher was doubtful, but she decided to let them try. If Ron were still hoarse tomorrow, at least they'd have a back-up plan. At first, Rich read too fast, but with some practice, the boys were soon able to do the trick perfectly. It was impossible to tell that Rich was the voice behind Ron's lips.

The next day, Ron came to school with the same whispery voice as before. The back-up plan had been kept secret so that the audience would not be thinking about that instead of just enjoying the play. Everyone wondered if people would be fooled.

After a fine production, people came up to Ron to say what a good voice he had! Ron would smile in silence. Rich, on the other hand, figured the secret didn't need to be kept anymore. Besides, he thought it was time to have some fun again. When he began to talk for his twin, there were some startled looks, and soon the whole truth came out!

DIRECTIONS Find and circle a word in the story to answer each question. Write the word on the line.

What is the homonym for

1. *knot* that means "in no way"? _____

2. *wood* that is the past tense of "will"? _____

3. *site* that means "able to see"? _____

4. *sighed* that is one of three lines of a triangle? _____

5. *cruise* that is a group of people working together? _____

6. *horse* that means "a gruffness of the voice"? _____

7. *red* that means "gained knowledge from books"? _____

8. *close* that names what people wear? _____

9. *sum* that is not a definite number? _____

10. *caws* that means "make something happen"? _____

11. *knead* that means "what one wants or must have"? _____

12. *reed* that means "to say the words in a book"? _____

13. *seen* that is the place where something happens? _____

14. *hole* that means "all of something"? _____

15. *they're* that shows ownership? _____

16. *stair* that means "to look at without blinking"? _____

REMEMBER Check for spelling and meaning when words sound alike.

Making the Most of It

Have you ever needed a letter you threw away by accident? When you found it, you probably had a hard time figuring out the message. You had to use the words you could read to help you figure out the ones you couldn't.

In this lesson, you will use what you know to figure out what you don't know. You will read about people who made the most from what they had.

1 KEYS to Context

The meaning of a whole sentence or paragraph is called context.

LEARN You can use the words you know to help with words you don't know.

> Millie hoped to win Honorable Mention if she couldn't win first, second, or third prize.

To figure out what honorable mention is, use the rest of the paragraph. You can understand from the other words in the paragraph that Honorable Mention must be an award for an entry that is very good, even if it does not win first, second, or third prize.

DIRECTIONS Use what you can read of this smudged and torn note to figure out what the writer was saying. Fill in the missing words or parts of words.

> Dear Terry,
>   Thank you for invit_____ _____ to spend the holidays at your ski lodge. I wil_____ve by train on the Wed_____ before Thanksgiving at 3:30 p._____
>   Will you be able to p_____ up at the station or should I pla_____ take a taxi?
>   Since_____
>   John

2 Practice With Context

DIRECTIONS The same underlined word appears in each group of sentences. It does not mean the same thing in all three sentences. Draw a line through the sentence in each group in which the underlined word has a different meaning.

1. The science <u>club</u> meets after school at 3:30.
   Everyone in the garden <u>club</u> had to bring flowers.
   The man was practicing with his golf <u>club</u>.

2. The snowman contest was held in the <u>park</u>.
   Mother could not find a place to <u>park</u> her car.
   Christy and Michelle went to the <u>park</u> for a picnic.

3. Louise bought a new <u>record</u> for her stereo.
   The team has an impressive <u>record</u> this year.
   Dorothy dropped the <u>record</u> as she was getting ready to play it.

4. The moonlight was so <u>bright</u> we could see without a light.
   The <u>bright</u> headlights helped us see in the dense fog.
   Kira's friends knew she was <u>bright</u> when she won the spelling contest.

5. The <u>stump</u> is what is left after a tree is chopped down.
   Can you <u>stump</u> your friends with a card trick?
   The sled hit the <u>stump</u> and tipped over.

6. We <u>ground</u> up the vegetables in the food processor.
   The gopher ran into a hole in the <u>ground</u>.
   The beef was <u>ground</u> into hamburger for the barbecue.

Read and Apply

The snow finally stopped falling early Saturday morning. At 120 Maple Street Ted thought breakfast would take forever. By the time he and his sister Cassie burst out the front door, they could already hear excited shouts from the park a block away.

"Ted, look! The snow is up to my knees!" Cassie giggled as she fell into the soft whiteness. "I can't move!"

"Hey, Ted!" called a voice from the yard next door.

"Wait till you hear this." Pete pushed through the snow quickly.

"There's a snowman contest at the park! Real prizes, too." Pete brushed some snow out of his dark hair. "Judging's at noon."

The two boys grinned. "Let's go!" shouted Pete.

Ted glanced at Cassie. "You can come, too," he said over his shoulder. "You can help us."

The park was already crowded. Pete, Ted and Cassie moved to an open area on the far side and got to work.

Very soon they had a sizable snowman, complete with pinecone eyes and a holly berry mouth.

"He needs a hat. How about yours?" asked Pete. "We don't have time to go home for anything."

"OK," Ted answered and pulled his wool cap over the snowman's head.

The three stepped back to admire their creation.

"Look out!" shouted a voice. A flash of red was careening down the hill straight toward them!

Whump!

Cassie slowly uncovered her eyes. Their beautiful snowman was once more three uneven balls of snow. A sled lay on its side, and a boy in a red jacket was carefully getting to his feet.

"Don't you know this is the new sled run?" the boy asked. "What are you doing here?"

"Trying to win a contest," Ted answered glumly.

"The snowman contest," Pete added. He pointed to the other side of the park, where two judges were already stopped in front of the first snow figure.

Another sled whizzed by.

"Look, you can't stay here," said the boy in the red jacket. "Use my sled, and move your snowman over near that tree." Working in pairs, they hoisted the balls of snow onto the sled and headed for the tall pine.

They were nearly there when Cassie felt the sled jerk and then tip over, stopped by an old stump they hadn't seen. The balls of snow were once more on the ground. This time they lay neatly together, with Ted's cap covering the snowman's face.

"Oh, no," groaned Pete and Ted together.

Cassie heard footsteps and looked up.

"And what have we here?" one of the judges asked.

Cassie gave the overturned sled a disappointed kick. "I guess our snowman got tired of sledding and just fell asleep," she said.

The judges looked at each other. Then one of them put his fingers to his lips. "Shh . . . ," he said. The other placed a shiny ribbon on the sleeping snowman. The ribbon read "Honorable Mention for the Most Original Snowman on Sled Hill."

DIRECTIONS Find each of the underlined words in the story. Then circle the word that best tells the meaning of the underlined word.

1. <u>burst</u>

walked   rushed   fell

2. <u>soft whiteness</u>

snow   ice   feathers

3. <u>careening</u>

revolving   walking   swerving

4. <u>hoisted</u>

kicked   rolled   raised up

5. <u>glumly</u>

happily   sadly   angrily

6. <u>sizable</u>

tiny   funny   big

REMEMBER Context helps you figure out unfamiliar words.

Trouble at Rendezvous

Do you know the meaning of the word *yield*? If you read "yields three dozen" in a cookie recipe, you can figure out that *yields* means "gives up" or "gives out."

In this lesson, you will learn to use the words around an unknown word to help you understand its meaning. You'll read about a bully who was forced to yield when he met more than his match.

1 KEYS to Context Clues

Words you know help you understand words you don't know.

LEARN You can figure out the meaning of a new word even if you can't pronounce it. Read the paragraph to find the meaning of *rendezvous*.

In the 1800s hunters and trappers who lived in the area that is now Colorado and Wyoming had an annual rendezvous. It was usually held in June or July. People who hadn't seen one another for years would congregate to trade goods, tell stories, play games, and just have a good time. A rendezvous could last several weeks. For hunters and trappers who lived in solitude most of the year, the summer rendezvous was a great chance for visiting.

Even though you may not be able to say *rendezvous*, you probably figured out that a *rendezvous* is a gathering, or a meeting. *Rendezvous* (pronounced RON-DAY-VOO) is borrowed from the French language.

DIRECTIONS Use the context of the paragraph to match words with their definitions. Write the letter of the correct definition on the line.

a. yearly   **b.** being alone   **c.** get together

_____ 1. congregate   _____ 2. annual   _____ 3. solitude

Practice With Context Clues

DIRECTIONS Use context to figure out the meaning of the underlined word in each sentence. Circle its definition.

1. The <u>surplus</u> paint allowed us to paint another room after all.

    can   extra   handful

2. Mary thought her friend Hilda was a <u>manipulator</u> since Hilda was so clever about getting others to do whatever she wanted.

    plant   inspector   controller

3. The view from the top of the grand canyon is <u>picturesque</u>, like a beautiful painting.

    like a picture   distasteful   ugly

4. Roberto was quite <u>affable</u>, and everyone in the class liked him.

    mean   unfriendly   friendly

5. The candle had become <u>distorted</u> when it melted in the hot sun.

    fancy   out of shape   unused

6. The <u>vast</u> football stadium held over 100,000 people.

    enormous   hidden   small

7. The <u>ravenous</u> bear was eating everything in sight.

    angry   starving   huge

8. We <u>amended</u> our rules after seeing that some of them didn't work out.

    improved   printed   liked

DIRECTIONS Read to find out how Buller the bully met his match. Use context to figure out the definitions of any words you don't know.

The lonely hunters and trappers led isolated lives in the Rocky Mountains. The annual summer rendezvous offered them a time to socialize and the opportunity to trade the wares they had worked on during the long winter. Spirits were high as people came from all parts, anticipating a good time.

One giant-like man was not welcome at the rendezvous. He always showed up, though, and wherever Buller went, calamity followed. Everyone detested Buller. He was a notorious braggart and bully. His stories were embellished to the point of

being ridiculous. He provoked fights and delighted in picking on the smallest men around. Buller didn't know what lay in store for him this year.

By the first evening of the rendezvous, it was already obvious who Buller had selected as his prey. Young Mort, who was half Buller's size, was the newest trapper in the bunch. He had come to the gathering alone. Buller took it upon himself to welcome the newcomer.

"Look at this here yellow-bellied half-pint!" bellowed Buller, slapping Mort on the back so hard that the smaller man went soaring into a circle of dancers.

"I will break you in two, then you'll be twice the man you was!" snorted the bully.

Knowing a showdown was coming, the dancers became silent. The music stopped. Buller towered over Mort, who was staggering to his feet. Buller didn't hesitate. He grabbed Mort by the hair and picked him off the ground. He prepared to swing Mort by his hair.

Just then three strangers appeared out of nowhere. Each man was as huge as Buller. As they stood in front of the bully with their arms folded, they almost appeared as one man rather than three. They did not speak. They only stood, statue-like, and stared into Buller's eyes.

Buller's gasp was audible to the crowd. He slowly lowered Mort to the ground. Then, without a sound, the three strangers hoisted a kicking, yelling Buller onto their shoulders. They carried him out to the watering trough, and dumped him in.

Buller picked himself up. He slunk away. After that, no one ever had to be afraid of Buller again. He had met his match.

DIRECTIONS Find each numbered word in the story, and underline it. Use context to help you write the correct definition on the line.

1. embellished _____ hated

2. provoked _____ able to be heard

3. prey _____ trouble

4. isolated _____ one who is helpless

5. notorious _____ exaggerated

6. audible _____ one who boasts

7. socialize _____ caused to happen

8. braggart _____ known for bad deeds

9. detested _____ talk with others

10. calamity _____ far from others

DIRECTIONS Use some of the numbered words to complete the sentences.

1. I know now I was a _____ when I _____ the story of my good deed.

2. Bullies are _____ by their _____.

REMEMBER Think about the context when you come to an unfamiliar word.

Inviting Islands

Jake's mother told him to lay his homework papers on the kitchen island. Will Jake's homework be surrounded by water? In this lesson, you'll learn about words like *island* that have more than one meaning as you read about some inviting islands in the world.

1 KEYS to Multiple-Meaning Words

Many words have more than one meaning.

LEARN When a word has more than one meaning, we use the words around it to find out which meaning was used. Look at the meanings of *invite*:

1. ask politely to come to some place or to do something
2. attract or tempt
3. (tend to cause)

In the sentence, *This island is so inviting that we'd like to stay forever,* the other words tell us that *inviting* means *attract or tempt.*

DIRECTIONS Read the paragraph. Then circle the best meaning for each underlined word below.

Catalina Island <u>sits</u> twenty-three miles off the <u>coast</u> of California. People enjoy Catalina Island's unspoiled beauty. There are many <u>rare</u> animals and birds on the island that cannot be found anywhere else.

Sits means: 1. perches   2. (is located)   3. rests on the lower part

Rare means: 1. (seldom found)   2. not cooked   3. not happening often

Coast means: 1. (land along the sea)   2. slide without using power

2 Practice With Multiple Meanings

DIRECTIONS Use the words around each underlined word to decide which dictionary definition below is the best meaning for the sentence. Write its number on the line.

fig ure 1. a shape, outline, or form 2. a picture or diagram 3. a person thought of in a certain way 4. a number

de gree 1. a step in a series or progress of something 2. a unit used in measuring temperature 3. a rank earned by a student who completes a course of study

bridge 1. something built over water or a low area 2. the upper, bony part of the nose 3. a small frame for false teeth that is fastened to real teeth

crown 1. a head piece of gold or jewels worn by royalty 2. first place in a contest 3. the top part of the head 4. the part of the tooth that sticks out from the gum

horse 1. a large animal with four legs, solid hoofs, and a mane and tail 2. a frame on legs for supporting things 3. a padded block on legs used in gymnastic exercises

_3_ 1. The dentist put a <u>bridge</u> in her mouth.

_3_ 2. My mom won't have homework after she gets her <u>degree</u> in June.

_2_ 3. You can draw stick <u>figures</u> for the people, if you like.

_2_ 4. I'll just put this wood up on the <u>horses</u> to saw it.

_1_ 5. The queen wore a <u>crown</u>.

_1_ 6. There aren't any <u>horses</u> in the pasture.

_2_ 7. I fell and smacked the <u>bridge</u> of my nose.

_2_ 8. The temperature has risen a few <u>degrees</u> since noon.

_3_ 9. Grandpa is a respected <u>figure</u> in our family.

_1_ 10. We'll get this project done, one <u>degree</u> at a time.

_1_ 11. The <u>bridge</u> was out, so we went around the lake.

_3_ 12. He worked out on the <u>horse</u> in gym today.

_2_ 13. My favorite boxer won the heavyweight <u>crown</u>.

_4_ 14. The <u>figures</u> in the chart tell how many books were read.

_3_ 15. His head was totally bald in the <u>crown</u>.

_1_ 16. These <u>figures</u> are all triangles.

_4_ 17. My dad saw the dentist to have a <u>crown</u> replaced.

3 Read and Apply

DIRECTIONS Look for words with multiple meanings as you read about two interesting islands.

Manhattan Island is a long, narrow island in New York City's harbor. About 1½ million people live on this island of sharp differences. Some of the country's richest people live in Manhattan's beautiful and luxurious upper east side. In spite of this wealth, you do not have to go very far on the island to find crowded apartments occupied by some of the poorest people in the United States.

The skyscrapers in Manhattan make the streets look like deep gorges. People can walk for miles with nothing but cement under their feet. However, the island's huge Central Park has plenty of grass, trees, fields, and rolling hills for recreation.

Another interesting island is located in the waters near the Straits of Mackinac, a narrow body of water that connects Lake Huron and Lake Michigan. Native American Indians lived on Mackinac Island long before the first Europeans arrived. During the American Revolution and in the War of 1812, the island changed hands many times. France, Britain, and the United States fought for control of the island. At some point, each of the countries owned it.

After the United States gained ownership, a wealthy fur trader, John Jacob Astor, set up his company's headquarters on Mackinac Island. In 1894, the United States federal government transferred much of the island to the state of Michigan. Most of this land is now a state park.

No cars or trucks are allowed on the island today. People get there by ferry boats that run from the mainland. Once there, tourists travel on horses or bicycles.

Find and circle in the article you just read, each of the words listed below. Use the whole sentence to decide each word's meaning. Read the groups of meanings below and write the correct word on the line above each group. Then circle the meaning used in the article. The first one is done for you.

A. ~~gorges~~	D. ~~rolling~~	H. ~~point~~
B. ~~sharp~~	E. ~~connects~~	I. ~~allowed~~
C. ~~cement~~	F. ~~hands~~	J. ~~run~~
	G. ~~control~~	

1. point
   a. sharp end
   b. the main idea
   c. (a certain time)

2. run
   a. score in baseball
   b. go by moving the legs quickly
   c. keep going

3. allowed
   a. permitted
   b. given
   c. made up for something

4. hands
   a. end parts of the arms
   b. pointers on a clock
   c. control

5. control
   a. grasp or grip
   b. ownership or use of
   c. hold back or curb

6. gorges
   a. greedily stuffs with food
   b. narrow passes or valleys
   c. throats or gullets

7. cement
   a. to make stronger
   b. surface of lime and clay mixed with water and sand

8. rolling
   a. traveling on wheels
   b. smoothly laid out, one after another

9. connects
   a. brings together
   b. thinks of at the same time
   c. plugs into electrical circuit

10. sharp
    a. having thin cutting edge
    b. clear or easily seen
    c. a musical half step higher

REMEMBER The meaning of a multiple-meaning word depends on its use.

Geometry And More

Have you ever had someone give you more information than you really wanted? In this lesson, you'll learn about words with multiple meanings as you read about a boy who got more help than he asked for.

1 KEYS to Multiple-Meaning Words

A word can have more than one meaning.

LEARN   Many words have multiple meanings. This means they have more than one meaning. When you read such a word, you decide its meaning by the way it is used.

EXAMPLE   The word *line* has many different meanings.

U. a rope or string
V. a row
M. a letter or note

L. a long, narrow mark
E. to cover the inner surface of
O. a system of wires connecting telephones

DIRECTIONS Write the letter of the correct definition before each sentence. You will spell a word used in the story in this lesson.

___V___ **1.** The teacher asked us to get in *line*. ✓

___O___ **2.** The telephone *line* is busy. ✓

___L___ **3.** Put a *line* under the correct answer. ✓

___M___ **4.** Throw me the *line* so I can tie up the boat. ✓

___U___ **5.** Write me a *line* when you have time. ✓

___E___ **6.** We need to *line* the litter box with newspaper. ✓

Practice With Multiple-Meaning Words

Read the sentences and definitions. Write each sentence's number on the line before the best definition of the underlined word.

1. See if you can <u>draw</u> a picture of a dog.

2. We will each <u>draw</u> three cards from the deck.

    _1_ **a.** to make a picture or design ✓

    _2_ **b.** to select or choose ✓

3. There are many <u>tables</u> in the cafeteria.

4. I need to practice my multiplication <u>tables</u>.

    _4_ **a.** an orderly list of facts or figures ✓

    _3_ **b.** furniture with flat surfaces and four legs ✓

5. A valentine has the <u>shape</u> of a heart.

6. My bike is in bad <u>shape</u>.

    _6_ **a.** condition ✓

    _5_ **b.** form or figure ✓

7. What is the <u>object</u> of the game?

8. A piano is a heavy <u>object</u> to move.

    _8_ **a.** article or thing ✓

    _7_ **b.** a purpose or goal ✓

9. There was no <u>space</u> on the bus to sit down.

10. The sun and stars are in outer <u>space</u>.

    _9_ **a.** open area ✓

    _10_ **b.** the region beyond the earth's atmosphere ✓

Read and Apply

DIRECTIONS Note the underlined words as you read about Vince's lesson.

Vince burst into the kitchen and dropped his arithmetic book on the table in disgust. "I'll never understand this geometry stuff!" he grumbled.

"Do you have a problem with some problems, Little Brother?" Ashley chimed.

"Very funny!" said Vince, annoyed with his sister's tone of voice.

"I said that for a reason, Vince," remarked his sister quickly. "Notice how I used the word *problem* in two different ways."

"Okay, but your playing with words doesn't help me figure out how to do this assignment!"

"Maybe not, but we can have some fun in the process. Listen to the word you just used. *Figure* can mean different things. You can write a figure 3 or draw a figure of a cat. Then there's the president who is an important figure."

"Let's look at *figure,* as in figuring out the area of a figure," said her brother.

"Now you're catching on," Ashley said with a grin. "Notice, Vince, that each of these figures is a plane figure."

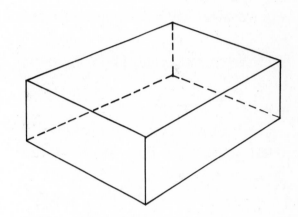

"They don't look like airplanes to me," Vince giggled.

"I knew you'd say that, but in this case, *plane* means a flat <u>surface</u>. This door is a plane figure. To find the area of the door's surface, you multiply its height by its width."

"Okay," said Vince. "The door is six feet high and three feet wide. That's . . . uh . . . eighteen feet."

"Almost," said Ashley, "but you have to say 'square' feet. That's because you can actually draw eighteen squares inside the area of the door's surface. All sides of each square would be one foot long. Here, let me show you." Ashley quickly sketched a rectangle. Then she drew lines inside the rectangle so there were eighteen squares.

"All right, I think I understand what area means now," said Vince, "but what about *volume?*"

"Volume . . . hmmm . . . there's another fun word, Vince. You can turn down the volume of the radio, hand me an encyclopedia volume, or find the volume of a box."

"There you go again, but I think the box is the one I need," said Vince.

"Well, to find the volume or amount of space inside a box, you multiply the box's length times its width times its height. Volume is always in cubic units because . . . Vince, where are you going?"

"To do this homework so I can go out to play. Thanks, Sis!"

DIRECTIONS Read each pair of sentences. Place a check mark before the sentence that uses the underlined word in the same way it was used in the story.

1. __✓__ The surface of the desk is very dirty.

   _____ The whale will surface very soon.

2. _____ You can always get a square meal at Grandma's house.

   __✓__ My room is nearly a perfect square.

3. __✓__ What is the area of your back yard?

   _____ I'm sure that he lives somewhere in this area.

4. _____ The class chose sides for their game.

   __✓__ One of the sides on this figure is missing.

REMEMBER Use the sentence to decide which meaning to choose.

A Long Race

Who is the fastest runner in your class? You can find out by having a race. In this lesson, you will read about a very long race called a marathon. You will also learn how to use clues to help you figure out the correct meaning of a word.

 1 ## KEYS to Multiple-Meaning Words

A word can be used to mean different things.

LEARN   When you read a word that has more than one meaning, you can use the rest of the sentence or the paragraph to give you clues to the right meaning. These clues are called *context clues.*

EXAMPLE   Before she celebrated, Joan ran one last *lap.* You know that Joan went around a racecourse because the rest of the sentence gave you clues to the meaning of *lap.*

DIRECTIONS   Read each sentence. Write the letter of the correct meaning on the line.

_____ **1.** My track *coach* has spent many hours helping me learn to run.
   a. large, closed carriage
   b. person who teaches and trains others

_____ **2.** Each year thousands of runners participate in a famous long distance *race* called the Boston Marathon.
   a. large group of human beings
   b. a contest of speed

② Practice With Multiple–Meaning Words

DIRECTIONS Look at each underlined word and its definitons. Read the sentences and write the number of the best meaning for the underlined word in each sentence. Remember to use context clues.

_____ Eva ran the <u>course</u> in record time.

_____ The final <u>course</u>, dessert, is always my favorite.

_____ The boat was off <u>course</u> because of the storm.

    1. a way or path along which someone or something moves
    2. a part of a meal served at one time
    3. the direction taken

_____ The <u>runner</u> keeps the wooden hall floor clean and warm.

_____ Before the race, each <u>runner</u> pinned a number on her shirt.

_____ The shiny <u>runners</u> made patterns on the ice.

    1. a person who runs
    2. a long, narrow cloth or rug
    3. the blade of an ice skate or sled

_____ The runners must <u>train</u> for several weeks before a long distance race.

_____ Hurry before the <u>train</u> leaves the station!

_____ The flower girls carried the <u>train</u> of the bride's gown.

    1. get fit by proper diet, exercise and practice
    2. a part that hangs down and drags along
    3. connected line of railroad cars moving along together

3. Read and Apply

DIRECTIONS Read about how marathons began.

Long ago, people were trained to run long distances to carry news from one place to another. During times of war, runners <u>carried</u> messages to and from battlefields. If a victory was won, a runner raced <u>back</u> to the city to spread the good news. If there were problems, a runner was sent back to call for extra help.

In the year 490 B.C., the Athenians of Greece were fighting the Persians in a battle at a place called Marathon. It was about 25 miles from Marathon to the city of Athens.

When the Athenian army defeated the Persians at Marathon, a runner was sent back to Athens with the news. Along with the good news, this runner had to warn the people that the Persians were going to attack again. This time they were planning to sail along the coast and attack Athen's harbor. The runner ran the 25 miles as fast as he could. When he reached the city, he gave his message of victory. Then he raced to the harbor before the Persians landed. Although his effort cost him his life, the city and its people were saved. In honor of this runner, certain long distance races are now called marathons.

Over the years, the distance of the marathon has changed. It was increased from 25 miles to about 26

miles when the modern Olympic Games began in 1896. In 1904, the distance of the marathon was changed again, because the queen of England wanted to see the finish of the race from her royal box seat. The <u>finish</u> line was <u>moved</u> ahead 385 yards so it would be <u>right</u> in front of the queen's seat. Today, the marathon is a race that is 26 miles and 385 yards.

Use context clues to circle the letter of the correct meaning of each underlined word from the article you just read.

1. <u>carried</u>   **a.** taken from one place to another

   b. transferred a number from one place in the sum to another

   c. held up or supported

2. <u>back</u>   **a.** the opposite of front

   b. the place where one came from

   c. a football player whose position is behind the line

3. <u>finish</u>   **a.** a certain surface given by painting

   b. to use up

   c. to come to an end

4. <u>moved</u>   **a.** changed the place where one lives

   b. went forward

   c. changed the place or position

5. <u>right</u>   **a.** in a straight line, directly opposite

   b. agrees with the facts

   c. the opposite of left

DIRECTIONS Think about the other meanings of the words above. Write the correct definition on the line to tell the meaning of the underlined word in each sentence.

1. The runner in the <u>back</u> of the line raced forward.

   _____

   _____

2. He ran on the <u>right</u> side of the track.

   _____

   _____

3. He might need to be <u>carried</u> after the race.

   _____

   _____

4. A wet glass will damage the <u>finish</u> of the table.

   _____

   _____

REMEMBER A word's meaning depends on the context.

40 Multiple-Meaning Words

Dollars and Cents

You've probably heard someone say "money doesn't grow on trees." It means that money should be used wisely because it must be earned through work. In this lesson, you'll read about money as you learn about some shortened words.

1 KEYS to Contractions

Contractions combine two words.

LEARN A contraction is formed when a word and part of another word are combined. An apostrophe represents the missing letters.

EXAMPLE The bank is closed, so I cannot cash this check today.

The *bank's* closed, so I *can't* cash this check today.

Bank and *is* are combined to form the contraction *bank's*. The apostrophe stands for the *i* that was left out. The letters *no* are replaced by an apostrophe to form the contraction *can't*.

DIRECTIONS On the line before each contraction, write the letter of the two words used to make that contraction. Draw a line through letter or letters that have been left out of the contraction. The first one is done for you.

_C_ 1. what's	_____ 5. hasn't	**A.** has not	**E.** they have
_____ 2. they've	_____ 6. where's	**B.** could have	**F.** were not
_____ 3. could've	_____ 7. she's	**C.** what i̶s	**G.** she is
_____ 4. weren't	_____ 8. you'll	**D.** where is	**H.** you will

DIRECTIONS Read each sentence, and circle the contraction. On line *a*, write the two words from which the contraction was made. Write the letter or letters left out of the contraction on line *b*.

1. When paper money is worn out or damaged, it's shredded and burned.

   a. _____

   b. _____

2. In the last century, dirty money wasn't destroyed. It was washed, ironed, and reused.

   a. _____

   b. _____

3. There's a picture of a president on every coin minted today.

   a. _____

   b. _____

4. George Washington didn't want his picture on coins, but many years after his death, it was used on the quarter.

   a. _____

   b. _____

5. The United States has a law that the picture of a living person can't be on a money bill.

   a. _____

   b. _____

6. It'd take a person twenty years of sixteen-hour working days to count a billion dollars in United States dollar bills.

   a. _____

   b. _____

7. Coins in the United States don't have numbers on them to show the amounts. The amounts are written in words.

   a. _____

   b. _____

3 Read and Apply

DIRECTIONS Read about the history of coins. Then circle each contraction.

Needless to say, money doesn't grow on trees! It took many years for money to become what we know and use today.

Long ago when there weren't any coins or bills, people traded to buy things they wanted. Nails, shells, salt, and many other items, including animals were traded. People found, however, that it wasn't easy to make change. You couldn't split a hog or a horse! Besides, hauling a large animal around must've been difficult. Another problem was that if the other person didn't want what you had, there'd be no way to trade. A common object used for buying things was definitely needed.

The first coins were used around 2500 B.C. in Egypt, but they weren't used alone. A coin and a handful of beans might've bought a pair of shoes then. Another thousand years later, some people decided that a standard form of coins should be used. Gold and silver were selected for making coins because they're valuable metals which are strong and lightweight.

Early coins weren't much like what's used today. Some of the earliest Chinese coins were in the shape of tools. The Greeks treated each coin as a piece of art, showing one of several beautifully-made symbols. One of the earliest attempts to prevent counterfeiting was begun around 300 B.C. by the Romans. They introduced the ridges on the edges of coins. This discouraged people from trying to cut coins in an attempt to change their appearance and value.

DIRECTIONS Read each sentence and the words in parentheses. Use the words in parentheses to write a contraction on the line to complete each sentence.

1. A _____ worth its full value if three fifths of it is undamaged. (bill is)

2. If more than three fifths of a paper bill is damaged, it _____ worth anything. (is not)

3. _____ about 13 billion coins minted in the United States each year. (There are)

4. Unlike most paper, _____ no wood pulp in the paper used to make paper money. (there is)

5. Dollar bills _____ expected to last for more than twenty-two months. (are not)

6. A nickel _____ now worth five cents was once worth one cent. (that is)

7. _____ part of the Secretary of Treasury's job to design paper money. (It is)

8. The general public _____ use bills larger than $100, since only banks use them. (does not)

9. If 257,588,120 dollar bills were laid end to end, _____ go all the way around the equator. (they would)

10. Once a coin's design is adopted, it _____ be changed for twenty-five years unless a special law is passed. (cannot)

11. When people _____ spend coins, a coin shortage can occur. (do not)

12. Paper money became necessary because people _____ stop hoarding, or keeping, coins. (would not)

13. Although wooden nickels _____ used long because they were considered illegal, they helped a bit during a severe coin shortage. (were not)

REMEMBER A contraction is a shortened form of two words.

Games to Play

How many different games can you name? Which ones do you like to play? In this lesson, you'll read about some games as you learn about compound words.

 ## KEYS to Compound Words

A compound word is made from two shorter words.

LEARN A compound word is a shortcut. It expresses an idea in one word that would otherwise take several words. When you see a compound word, it is usually easy to figure out its meaning by separating it into its two shorter words.

EXAMPLE *Wallpaper* uses less words than *paper that is pasted on a wall. Phonebooth* is a compound word for *a booth that holds a phone.*

DIRECTIONS Separate each compound word into two words by drawing a slash mark. Then complete the meaning of the compound word by writing its two shorter words. The first one is done for you.

1. d o g h o u s e   a <u>house</u> for a <u>dog</u>

2. t a b l e c l o t h   a _____ for a _____

3. r i v e r b a n k   a _____ of a _____

4. m o t o r b o a t   a _____ with a _____

5. b l u e b i r d   a _____ that is _____

Practice With Compound Words

DIRECTIONS Use the clues to make a compound word that fits each meaning. The first one is done for you.

1. Something that washes dishes.
   <u>dishwasher</u>

2. A container for shaking salt.
   _____

3. A cover that shields one from the wind.
   _____

4. Dust that comes from sawing wood.
   _____

5. A board on which scores are recorded.
   _____

6. Shelves that hold books.
   _____

DIRECTIONS In each sentence, underline the words that can be replaced by a compound word. Write the compound word on the line. The first one is done for you.

1. Dad used <u>paper with a sandy surface</u> to make the table smooth.
   <u>sandpaper</u>

2. Mom uses recipes from a book that tells about cooking.
   _____

3. Sally wants to be a person who keeps the books of figures.
   _____

4. My uncle's new sportscar has interesting caps that cover the wheel hubs.
   _____

5. Jackie went to the one who dresses her hair.
   _____

DIRECTIONS Look for compound words as you read about some games that are played with a ball.

Many words are invented because of new ideas or new discoveries. Some words were created because new games were devised. The games of basketball, football, tetherball, baseball, kickball, and racquetball caused new words to be coined. Stickball, handball, and softball are other ballgames whose names became new words.

The first baseball players used a stick to hit the ball. Later the stick was called a bat. If the ball was hit far enough without being caught, the hitter could run to a series of safe stopping places that became known as bases. If the runner touched all the bases and came back to the starting place without being tagged, a point was scored. It was only a matter of time before the ball used in this game with bases became known as a baseball.

The earliest basketball players probably used a basket with the bottom cut out. Later, the basket was nailed to the side of a building or to a pole. Players scored points if they could throw a ball so it dropped through the basket. In time, large, round balls were made for this game. Even though real baskets have been replaced by hoops, the name basketball remained.

A football can be kicked with the foot or thrown with the hand. Even though a football is carried or thrown much more often than it is kicked, it is still called a football.

DIRECTIONS Other games and sports activities use compound words. Combine a word from the first column with a word from the second column to make a compound word that has something to do with a game or sport. Write one of the compound words on the line to complete each sentence below.

hop	board
leap	hook
sail	pads
shuffle	shoes
skate	boat
fish	ball
horse	scotch
volley	guards
shin	frog

1. _____ is a game where a ball is volleyed over a net.

2. A boat that moves by means of sails is a

   _____.

3. One player leaps over others who are leaning over close to the ground or floor in

   _____.

4. A _____ with bait will usually catch a fish.

5. Players hop around a figure drawn on the ground in the game of

   _____.

6. Wooden disks are shoved, or shuffled, along a flat surface into a scoring area in the game of

   _____.

7. _____ are worn to protect the lower front part of the legs when playing soccer or hockey.

8. In _____, players toss U-shaped pieces of metal at an iron stake driven into the ground.

9. _____ protect the blades of ice skates when you are not skating.

REMEMBER Several words can often be replaced by a compound word.

Incredible Creatures

Do you like to read scary stories? In this lesson, you'll read about some scary creatures as you learn about prefixes.

1 KEYS to Prefixes

A prefix at the beginning of a word changes the word's meaning.

LEARN   A prefix is a group of letters at the beginning of a word. Each prefix has its own meaning and changes the root word's meaning.

EXAMPLE   *Mis* means *wrong*. If you *mis*place something, you put it in the wrong place. The prefix *pre* means *before,* so a *pre*historic creature is one that lived before history was recorded. The prefixes *in, em,* and *im* can mean *in* or *on. In* and *im* can also mean *not.*

DIRECTIONS Write a word from the list at the right to complete each sentence.

1. We had a _____ over the story to see how much we knew about King Kong.

2. This story about a snow monster is surely a

   _____ .

3. Sometimes people think of a mummy as an

   _____ monster.

incredible

pretest

mistake

Practice With Prefixes

DIRECTIONS To *re*start an engine is to start it again, since the prefix means *again*. When one *un*fastens a latch, the latch is the opposite of being hooked. Read the sentences. Find and circle any word with the *re, in, em, mis, pre, un,* or *im* prefix.

1. A monster is any plant or animal that is misformed, or not normal.

2. The word *monster* comes from a Latin word which was used to prewarn of a coming misfortune.

3. Stories of giant shepherds, the Cyclops in Sicily, have been retold for centuries.

4. A Cyclops was incredibly ugly, since he had one eye in the middle of his forehead.

5. A small girl impresses the reader when she overcomes a bear, a witch, and the one-eyed Cyclops in Ogden Nash's poem, *The Adventures of Isabel.*

6. Frankenstein is the infamous and unsightly monster from Mary Shelley's well-known horror novel.

7. Actually, Frankenstein is the creator of the monster, but the monster has come to be called by its inventor's name.

8. Frankenstein rejects the monster he created because of its hideous appearance, and the monster seeks revenge.

9. Mary Shelley's horror story tells of her feelings that people sometimes misjudge others simply because of appearance.

10. I once read a monster tale that turned out to be a misprint.

Read and Apply

Look for words with prefixes as you read about more incredible creatures.

Monsters have long been popular, even with younger folks. Some television shows for preschoolers have harmless monsters, who misbehave now and then. One graduates quickly, however, from gentle monsters to more gruesome, incredible ones.

Vampires are monsters whose fame comes from folk tales. Vampires, it is said, embark on nighttime prowls, looking for blood from sleeping persons. Vampire bats take their name from the vampire creature, since these bats can only swallow liquids and do, in fact, feed on the blood of other living things.

In 1897, an English author named Bram Stoker wrote the most famous vampire story of all time. His character, Count Dracula, resided in Transylvania, Romania. People were so impressed by Stoker's novel that they flocked to see a movie version of it when *Nosferatu, the Vampire* was made in 1922 and again when *Dracula* was unveiled in 1931.

Monsters continue to attract readers and movie-goers, as witnessed by the popularity of a movie called *Jaws*, released in 1975. In the movie, the monster is a shark that attacks swimmers. Although shark attacks on people are not unknown, the story of Jaws embellished the monster. The actual star of the first movie and those that have followed, is an unreal mechanical form resembling a shark.

Find a word in the article you just read to match each definition sentence. Write the word on the line.

1. This word is the opposite of *held* and has a prefix which means *again.*

   _____

2. Children who are not yet in school are called by this word.

   _____

3. The root word means *one surface that is not an end,* and the prefix means *again.*

   _____

4. A word describing the opposite of doing what is right or what is expected is formed by adding a prefix meaning *wrong.*

   _____

5. The opposite of an actual thing or event can be expressed by adding a prefix meaning *not.*

   _____

6. This word, with a prefix that means *in* or *on,* means *to start out.*

   _____

7. When the thinking of people is affected, or when a mark such as a stamp is put on something, this word is used.

   _____

8. This word, whose root word has a homonym meaning *absolutely not,* tells about things that are not proven.

   _____

9. Bigfoot supposedly leaves a gigantic footprint, but some people think that story is best described by this word which means *not believable* or *hard to believe.*

   _____

10. In the old days, this word meant *to pull away a curtain to display something new.* Now it is used whenever something new appears.

    _____

11. This word may be used when witnesses to sightings of the Abominable Snowman in the Himalaya Mountains in Tibet believe what they have seen, but others think they exaggerate the facts.

    _____

12. The stories of the Abominable Snowman and of Bigfoot are much alike, and this word can be used to compare them.

    _____

REMEMBER A prefix is attached to the beginning of a word.

What Is Nessie?

What would you do if you were swimming or boating and suddenly saw something huge rise out of the water? In this lesson, you will read about what many people claim to have seen in a lake in Scotland. You will also learn about word endings, called suffixes.

 KEYS to Suffixes

A suffix can be added to the end of a word.

LEARN   A *suffix* is a group of letters attached to the end of a word. A suffix can change a word's meaning. Read each suffix and its meaning.

-less	without	-able	able to, capable or worthy of
-ness	state of being, quality of	-er	one who or something that
-ful	full of, filled with	-ly	in the manner of
-ize	to make to become		

DIRECTIONS Write the letter of each word's meaning to spell a mystery word.

_____ **1.** colorful   **O.** without color

_____ **2.** colorless   **S.** make formal

_____ **3.** worker   **R.** capable of being liked

_____ **4.** formalize   **E.** in a quick manner

_____ **5.** quickness   **N.** one who works

_____ **6.** quickly   **M.** filled with color

_____ **7.** likeable   **T.** state of being quick

② Practice With Suffixes

DIRECTIONS Add a suffix to each word to make a new word that fits the definition in parentheses. Then use the words to complete the sentences.

-less   -ness   -ful   -ize   -able   -er   -ly

A. teach_____ (one who teaches)

B. read_____ (capable of being read)

C. life_____ (without life)

D. pain_____ (filled with pain)

E. great_____ (state of being great)

F. slow_____ (in a slow manner)

G. modern_____ (make modern)

H. pleasant_____ (in a pleasant manner)

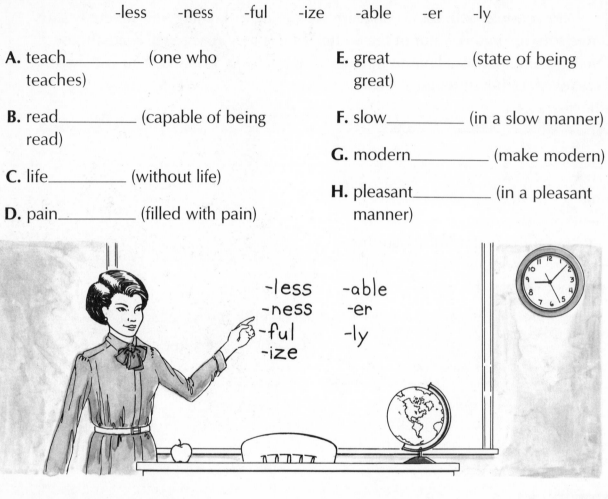

1. If you break a bone, it is a _____ experience.

2. My sister's handwriting is not _____.

3. Our class has a substitute _____ today.

4. You should walk _____ on ice.

5. A rock is a _____ object.

6. The children played _____ all morning.

7. They'll _____ the storefront to attract customers.

8. Not all good athletes are able to achieve _____.

Read and Apply

DIRECTIONS Think about the underlined words as you read about a famous monster.

Many people believe a strange creature lives in the water of Loch Ness, a long narrow lake in northern Scotland. Loch Ness is almost one thousand feet deep and very cold. The Loch Ness monster was supposedly first spotted in 1917. In that year, a girl and her brother were fishing from a boat when they saw the head of a huge monster break the surface of the water. Although the creature was moving <u>rapidly</u>, it did not try to chase the <u>youngsters</u>.

Because it was seen in Loch Ness, the monster came to be known as "Nessie." Since "Nessie" sounds like the name of a girl or woman, Nessie is often referred to as a "she-monster." Actually, Nessie could be either male or female. There may even be more than one Nessie.

Since 1917, there have been more than three thousand sightings of Nessie. Although some of these sightings have come from <u>reliable</u> witnesses, many of them have been <u>doubtful</u>. Scientists and <u>reporters</u> have tried to photograph Nessie, but because the pictures were taken under water, many have been fuzzy and poorly focused. Sonar recordings of the creature's noise have also given

uncertain results. For the most part, the search for scientific proof of Nessie's existence has been a <u>fruitless</u> one.

If Nessie really does exist, what is she? One idea is that she might be a gigantic snake. Another is that she is an enormous snail-like creature. Perhaps one of the most interesting theories, however, is that Nessie is a plesiosaur, a type of dinosaur that lived in the ocean millions of years ago.

There is a <u>remarkable</u> <u>likeness</u> between the plesiosaur and many of the photographs and descriptions of Nessie. If this idea is true, it would mean that not all plesiosaurs became extinct, or died out.

Each year more sightings of Nessie are reported, and more teams of scientists and <u>photographers</u>, using the most up-to-date equipment, search for her. Nessie, however, continues to outwit the scientists. Perhaps someday scientists will <u>realize</u> success. Until then, the monster called Nessie remains an unsolved mystery.

DIRECTIONS Choose an underlined word from the article for each meaning. Write the word on the line. Then use some of the words to complete the story.

1. able to be relied upon

_____

2. make real

_____

3. people who take pictures

_____

4. filled with doubt

_____

5. similarity

_____

6. in a fast manner

_____

7. people who report

_____

8. without results, without fruit

_____

9. worth being remarked about

_____

Newspaper _____ keep people informed about the latest Nessie sightings, some of which

seem to be from _____ witnesses. The search for scientific evidence has been a

_____ one, and many

scientists _____ that Nessie's existence is

_____ . Some people think Nessie might be a snake, or even a snail-like creature. Others

think she bears a _____ to the plesiosaur. Most witnesses agree that Nessie is huge and can

swim very _____ .

REMEMBER A suffix at the end of a word changes the word's meaning.

Strange Underwater Creatures

Fish and other animals that live in the water can come in many odd shapes and sizes. Some fish also have very unusual behavior. In this lesson, you'll read about some of these strange underwater creatures as you learn about root words.

 KEYS to Root Words

A root word is a word without a prefix of suffix.

LEARN   Many words are made up of several parts. Some words have prefixes. Some have suffixes. A *root word* has no prefix or suffix.

EXAMPLE   The underlined part of each word listed below is the root word. Notice the prefix before each root word in the first row. Each root word in the second row has a suffix.

un<u>cover</u>   mis<u>lay</u>   pre<u>pay</u>   re<u>build</u>   de<u>frost</u>   dis<u>able</u>
<u>quiet</u>ly   <u>sing</u>ing   <u>talk</u>ed   <u>kind</u>ness   <u>color</u>ful   <u>speech</u>less

DIRECTIONS   Read each word. Write its root word on the line.

1. misread _____
2. loudly _____
3. rewrite _____
4. unsure _____
5. sewed _____

6. disconnect _____
7. softness _____
8. decode _____
9. harmful _____
10. powerless _____

Practice With Root Words

DIRECTIONS The spelling of a root word is often changed when a suffix is added. If a root word ends in a silent *e*, like *please*, the e is dropped to form *pleasing* or *pleased*. The final consonant in the one-syllable root word *rob* is doubled before adding a suffix to form *robbing* or *robbed*.

Add each suffix to the word beside it. Write the new word on the line.

1. figure   +   ing   =   _____

2. flap   +   er   =   _____

3. close   +   est   =   _____

4. guide   +   ed   =   _____

5. quit   +   ing   =   _____

DIRECTIONS Read each sentence. Write the root of the underlined word on the line.

1. Many <u>unusual</u> creatures live under water.

_____

2. <u>Flying</u> fish have large fins.

_____

3. One type of perch can spend several hours on land <u>searching</u> for food.

_____

4. An electric eel can send <u>powerful</u> shocks to kill its food.

_____

5. A globefish, or puffer, fills up with air, <u>making</u> it look like a globe.

_____

6. Sharks will drown if they stop <u>swimming</u>.

_____

Read and Apply

DIRECTIONS Look for words with suffixes as you read about the sea anemone. Find a word in the story that ends with each suffix below. Write its root on the line.

One of the strangest sea creatures is the sea anemone. It does not look like an animal at all. Instead, its shape and colorful appearance make it look like a flower called the anemone. This, of course, is how it got its name.

The sea anemone has a body shaped like a tube. At one end of its body is a disk. The sea anemone uses the disk to attach itself to a rock or another object in the ocean. At the opposite end of its body is the sea anemone's mouth. This is surrounded by soft tentacles, or arms, that look like flower petals.

The sea anemone uses its tentacles to capture food. The tentacles throw out poison threads that paralyze tiny fish and other small sea animals. Then the sea anemone uses the tentacles to drag its prey into its mouth.

Sea anemones can be blue, green, red, pink, or a combination of several

colors. Although they are able to move, they do so very slowly. They usually stay attached to one object for several days before moving to another one. If the sea anemone is disturbed, it will pull in its tentacles and shorten its body. This makes it look like a lump on a rock.

1. ed _____

2. ed _____

3. ed _____

4. ed _____

5. ed _____

6. ly _____

7. ly _____

8. ing _____

9. ance _____

10. est _____

11. ful _____

12. en _____

Read about the Siamese fighting fish. Then write the root of each underlined word on a line. Find and circle each root in the hidden-word puzzle.

Another <u>interesting</u> underwater creature is the <u>fighting</u> fish, often called the Siamese fighting fish. It is a freshwater fish. Its native waters are clear rivers, lakes, and ponds in southeast Asia. It is a tiny fish, only <u>growing</u> to about two-and-one-half inches in length. The male's colors become very bright when it is <u>excited</u>.

The male fighting fish is a <u>quarrelsome</u> creature. Two males will <u>fight</u> each other until one of them is too <u>tired</u> to fight any longer. They dash at each other with <u>lightning</u> speed, biting and <u>tearing</u> each other's fins. Sometimes one of them is <u>killed</u>.

<u>Watching</u> fights between fighting fish is a popular sport in some areas of southeast Asia. Most wild fighting fish will stop fighting after about fifteen minutes, but people have <u>cultivated</u> some of the fish so their fights will last longer.

1. _____   5. _____   9. _____

2. _____   6. _____   10. _____

3. _____   7. _____   11. _____

4. _____   8. _____   12. _____

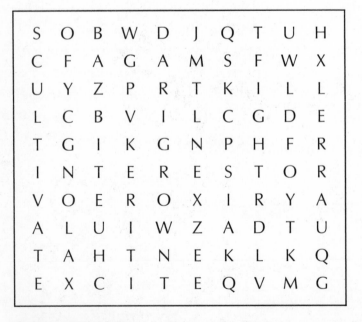

S	O	B	W	D	J	Q	T	U	H
C	F	A	G	A	M	S	F	W	X
U	Y	Z	P	R	T	K	I	L	L
L	C	B	V	I	L	C	G	D	E
T	G	I	K	G	N	P	H	F	R
I	N	T	E	R	E	S	T	O	R
V	O	E	R	O	X	I	R	Y	A
A	L	U	I	W	Z	A	D	T	U
T	A	H	T	N	E	K	L	K	Q
E	X	C	I	T	E	Q	V	M	G

REMEMBER A root word's meaning can be changed by a prefix or suffix.

Making the Right Choice

How did you decide what to wear today? You probably checked the weather outside and then compared all your clothes to see which would be most appropriate. You ruled out the sweaters if it was hot. In this lesson, you'll learn about a special kind of comparison. You'll read about how making comparisons helped in selecting a pet.

 ## KEYS to Analogies

An analogy is a comparison that shows two similar relationships.

LEARN   When we compare things, we think of how they are alike and different. Every day you make hundreds of choices, from which shirt to wear to when to do homework.

EXAMPLE   These shirts are both plaid.
I am tired now, but I will be rested after dinner.

You compare the shirts and find they are alike because they are both plaid. When you compare your feelings, you find a difference in how you feel now and how you will feel after dinner.

DIRECTIONS Read each sentence. Write *alike* or *different* on the line to tell how the underlined words are compared.

_____ 1. This hat and that cap are too hot to wear.

_____ 2. Mary is nine, but Alice is eleven.

_____ 3. A retriever is large, while a toy poodle is small

2 Practice With Analogies

DIRECTIONS A comparison is often written in the form of an analogy.

Morning is to evening as dawn is to dusk.

The first two underlined words have the same relationship as the last two under-lined words. That is, morning and evening are the beginning and ending of a day, just as dawn and dusk begin and end the day. Think of the relationship of a sofa and family room to complete this analogy:

Sofa is to family room as refrigerator is to _____.

A sofa is found in a family room, and a refrigerator is found in a kitchen. Think about each relationship. Write a word on the line to complete each analogy.

1. House is to people as barn is to _____.

2. Coats are to humans as _____ is to animals.

3. Swimsuit is to summer as coat is to _____.

4. Tadpole is to frog as _____ is to butterfly.

5. Saturday is to Sunday as March is to _____.

6. Child is to adult as _____ is to cat.

7. Disk is to computer as _____ is to tape recorder.

8. Egg is to chicken as milk is to _____.

9. Three is to tricycle as two is to _____.

3	**Read and Apply**

DIRECTIONS Read about how comparisons helped Brad make a wise decision.

Brad could hardly contain his excitement as he raced along, pausing only to push the shop door open to keep from smacking his nose on the glass.

"I want a puppy!" Brad breathlessly exclaimed.

"Well, you're panting as if a full-grown shepherd had chased you all the way here!" said the shopkeeper. "Why don't you catch your breath while I finish cleaning out this cage. Then we'll see what we can do for you. What breed of puppy is it you're wanting, anyway?"

"I want a big St. Bernard, but my dad says we can't keep such a large animal," said Brad rather sadly.

The door opened again as Brad's dad entered the shop. "Hello. I guess you can tell this guy's pretty anxious to take a pup home."

"Hello, I'm Jim. This fellow tells me he wants a big dog but that the rest of the family's not happy about his first choice." Jim looked at Brad. "Let's do a quick study of canine breeds and look at some of the needs of each. Then you should be able to make a choice that will meet with everyone's approval, including the puppy's!"

Jim led Brad and his dad to a corner of the shop where many books

lay neatly stacked on a shelf. Opening the books to pages of colored pictures, he said, "O.K., now let's see. There are about 128 recognized breeds of dogs. Some are pedigreed, which just means they're guaranteed to be the breed they're called. Then there are mixed breeds which are generally called mongrels or mutts. You can never tell what they'll look like when they're grown."

Analogies **63**

Jim went on to tell Brad that big dogs such as St. Bernards, sheepdogs, collies, German shepherds, Great Danes and retrievers require lots of space for living and exercise. He added that English toys, spaniels, Yorkshire terriers, chihuahuas, and toy poodles need little space and a lot less exercise.

Looking up at Jim, Brad said, "We live in an apartment and Dad and I are gone all day. I guess that means a St. Bernard is out. We probably need to get one of those small breeds that doesn't need a lot of attention."

"In that case," said Jim, "let's take a look at a few pups. Over here's a Boston terrier. He doesn't cause much trouble. In this cage is a basset hound who's friendlier than Santa Claus. Then there's this little pomeranian, that bulldog who's fast asleep over there. That little lady making all the fuss is a poodle."

Jim continued to name more of the puppies, but Brad had stopped listening the minute he set eyes on the basset hound who lay there so solemnly with its head resting on its paws. Brad noticed the burlap sack under the puppy.

"Sad Sack," he said. "That's what I'll call him. Hey, Dad! Can we buy Sad Sack? He just looks like he needs us."

As Brad and his Dad walked home with Sad Sack on his leash, Brad said thoughtfully, "Dad, maybe we should call him S.S. I don't think he's going to be very sad now that he has you and me. What do you think?"

DIRECTIONS Think about the comparisons in the story as you complete each of the analogies below.

1. Poodle is to apartment as _____ is to farmhouse.

2. Mongrel is to unknown as _____ is to known.

3. Chihuahua is to spaniel as St. Bernard is to _____.

4. Sad Sack is to S.S. as United States is to _____.

5. German shepherd is to English toy as _____ is to poodle.

REMEMBER An analogy is a kind of comparison.

The Tuxedo Bird

What bird looks as though it is wearing a tuxedo? In this lesson, you'll read about this interesting bird as you learn about a special way to compare relationships.

 ## KEYS to Analogies

An analogy is a way to show similar relationships.

LEARN An analogy shows two similar relationships. The first two words in an analogy have a relationship to each other. This same relationship is also found between the last two words in an analogy.

EXAMPLE Grass is to lawn as flower is to garden. Grass grows in a lawn just like a flower grows in a garden.

DIRECTIONS Write a word on the line to complete each analogy. Then complete the sentence to tell about the similar relationships.

1. Automobile is to roadway as _____ is to

   waterway. An automobile _____ a

   roadway just like a _____

   _____ a waterway.

2. Present is to today as future is to _____ .

   Today is in the _____ just like

   _____ is in the _____ .

Practice With Analogies

DIRECTIONS An analogy can be written as a sentence, or it can be written with a colon in place of the words *is to*. A double colon is then used in place of the word *as*. Read each analogy and circle the word that is needed to complete it. Write the word on the line to complete the analogy. Then write the analogy in its other form.

1. Child is to _____ as youth is to age.

    a. toddler   **b.** adult   **c.** animal   **d.** baby

    Child : _____ : : _____ : _____

2. Samantha is to female as Samuel is to _____ .

    a. male   **b.** Sam   **c.** human   **d.** somebody

    _____ : _____ : : Samuel : _____

3. Penguin is to bird as woman is to _____ .

    a. man   **b.** child   **c.** adult   **d.** human

    Penguin : _____ : : _____ : _____

4. Puck is to hockey as birdie is to _____ .

    a. tennis   **b.** baseball   **c.** badminton   **d.** jogging

    _____ : _____ : : birdie : _____

5. Whisper is to _____ as shout is to loudly.

    a. noise   **b.** yelling   **c.** calling   **d.** softly

    Whisper : _____ : : _____ : _____

Read and Apply

Read about some well-dressed birds.

A tuxedo is a man's dress suit. It is usually worn on very special, formal occasions. A tuxedo is usually not a part of a man's regular wardrobe. Most men rent the special suit for an occasion and return it afterward.

Not so with the penguin! This well-dressed bird, with its white breast and black back, seems to be in formal attire every day. Penguins live mainly in the Antarctic region, although a few are found in other parts of the world. Like a duck, a penguin's body is thickly covered with short feathers which secrete, or give off, an oil that serves as waterproofing. A thick layer of fat under the skin helps keep a penguin warm.

Emperor penguins waddle on their webbed feet. They are poor runners because their short legs are set far back on their bodies. Although penguins have short flipper-like wings that look like arms, they cannot fly. Instead, they use their wings and webbed feet as paddles for swimming as fast as twenty miles per hour.

A major difference between emperor and king penguins, the two most common groups of penguins, is that king penguins live in colonies on land. The emperor penguin never comes ashore. The female lays an egg on the ice, and the male keeps it warm for the two-month incubation period, or the time it takes to hatch. Both the male and female emperor have a flap of skin like a pocket near the top of their feet. They take turns keeping the egg warm by passing it from pocket to pocket with their feet.

Although the female helps out, the male penguin spends most of the time warming the egg. During this time, he fasts, or doesn't eat at all. When the egg hatches, he feeds crop, a substance from his throat, to the baby penguin. When the female returns from the ocean, the male goes into the ocean where he spends three weeks eating.

When all the male penguins return from their feasts, they and the females tightly surround all the pen- guin chicks for about six months. This keeps them warm until they get their own thick coats of oily feathers.

The main enemies of the penguin are the sea leopard and the Antarc- tica skua, a large, brown bird with white–tipped wings. The skua is about 22 inches long and has a strong beak. The penguin defends itself with its own beak or waddles away. It can also fall on its belly and push itself forward with its feet and wings.

DIRECTIONS Write a word from the story to complete each analogy. Then complete the same analogy in another way.

1. King penguin is to _____ as emperor penguin is to water.

   King penguin : _____ : : _____ : _____

2. Take is to give as _____ is to returned.

   _____ : _____ : : _____ : returned.

3. _____ is to formal as jeans are to informal.

   _____ : formal : : _____ : _____

4. Raincoat is to human as _____ are to penguin.

   _____ : _____ : : _____ : penguin

5. Milk is to newborn human as _____ is to newborn penguin.

   _____ : newborn human : :

   _____ : _____

6. Skuas are to penguins as _____ are to prey.

   _____ : _____ : : _____ : prey

REMEMBER Similar relationships are shown in an analogy.

68 Analogies

Nobody Liked Hilda

Would you be upset if your family didn't like your pet? In this lesson, you will read about a boy whose family did not like his pet hamster. You will learn about following directions.

1 KEYS to Following Directions

Directions help you save time and trouble.

LEARN You can save time and trouble when you understand the directions first. Special words can help you follow directions. Some of these special words are: *read, find, and underline.*

DIRECTIONS Read all the test items before you begin.

1. Write your name at the top of the page.
2. Circle the word *Hilda* in the lesson title.
3. Draw a happy face under your name.
4. Put your pencil down, and place your hands on your head.
5. Do only item 4. Ignore items 1, 2, and 3.

DIRECTIONS *Read* the paragraph. *Find* three things it tells you to do. *Underline* the three things.

To take good care of your new pet bird, do three things every day. Feed it once a day. Clean its cage every night. Cover its cage before you go to bed.

DIRECTIONS Read the story. Follow the direction under the picture.

Jill was excited. She had heard about fire drills from her big brother. Now, on only her third day of kindergarten, she was going to be in a fire drill herself! Jill and the other kindergarteners were excited. They tried very hard to listen to the teacher's directions. Here is what Mr. Martin said:

1. Never talk during a fire drill.

2. When you hear the file alarm bell, stop whatever you are doing.

3. Walk calmly to the door, and get in line.

4. Walk down the hall.

5. Turn right and go out the first exit.

When the fire bell rang, the kindergarten class was so excited that every child rushed to be first in line. The kindergarten class was the last class to leave the building. They were ashamed.

"Don't worry," said Mr. Martin. "We will do better next time. Next time you will remember all the directions."

Circle the number of the direction the kindergarten class forgot to follow.

Read and Apply

Read to find out how Marvin changed his family's mind about his pet hamster.

Hilda was Melvin's new hamster, and nobody liked Hilda. Melvin's father said she smelled. Melvin's mother said she was too noisy. And Melvin's sister Sheila said Hilda was stupid.

"She smells nice," said Melvin. "And she isn't noisy. Or stupid."

Melvin picked up Hilda. It was time to clean her cage. He took out the old wood shavings and put in new ones. Then he smelled the cage. It still smelled a little like Hilda.

Melvin took Hilda outside and sat under a rosebush. Melvin thought. How could he get his family to like Hilda?

Hilda twitched her nose. Melvin twitched his nose, too. He smelled the roses.

Suddenly Melvin had an idea. The roses smelled good. Melvin picked up a handful of rose petals. Then he went inside.

Melvin put Hilda and the rose petals in the cage. The rose petals looked pretty. Hilda piled them into a nest.

"Look!" Melvin said to his father.

"Mmmmm," he sniffed. "It smells good."

Hilda climbed onto her wheel. She ran forward. "SQUEAK!" went the wheel. She turned and ran the other way. "SQUEAK!" went the wheel again.

"Get Hilda to stop making that awful noise," said Melvin's mother.

"But, Mom," said Melvin, "Hilda needs her exercise."

Melvin picked up Hilda's wheel and turned it. "SQUEAK!"

"Look, Mom," said Melvin. "Hilda isn't noisy. It's her wheel. Could we fix it?"

"I think so," said Melvin's mother.

Melvin and his mother put some vegetable oil on the wheel. The squeaking stopped. Now Hilda could run as fast as she wanted and not make a sound.

"I still think she is a dumb pet," said Sheila. "All she does is eat and sleep and run on her wheel."

Hilda was part of Melvin's science fair project. But he didn't want anyone to know until it was finished.

Melvin built a maze with some blocks. There was only one way to get to the end.

At each correct turn Melvin put a sunflower seed. And Hilda really liked sunflower seeds. Soon she learned exactly which way to go, even when there weren't any seeds.

"Come one, come all!" said Melvin. "See the amazing Hilda do her marvelous trick!"

"I don't believe she can do a trick," said Sheila.

"Just watch," said Melvin.

He put Hilda down at the entrance to the maze. Everyone watched as she worked her way through it.

As Hilda finished they all clapped.

"I was wrong," said Sheila. "Hilda is a nice pet. And smart, too."

Melvin smiled and gave Hilda a sunflower-seed reward.

DIRECTIONS The directions that can help Melvin solve his hamster problems are all mixed up. Write them in order on the correct lines.

Put some oil on the wheel.
Put rose petals in the cage.
Turn the wheel to spread the oil.

Put in fresh wood shavings.
Get some vegetable oil.
Clean the cage.

How to Make Your Hamster Cage Smell Nice

_____ _____

_____ _____

_____

How to Keep Your Hamster Wheel Quiet

_____

_____

_____

REMEMBER Following directions correctly saves time.

Thomas Paine, Patriot

Thomas Paine's writing skills helped him become an important figure in America's fight for independence. In this lesson, you will read about Thomas Paine, an American patriot. You will learn to recognize the main idea and details of a paragraph.

1 KEYS to Main Idea and Details

The main idea is explained by the details.

LEARN The *main idea* of a paragraph tells what the paragraph is mainly about. A main idea is usually a sentence in the paragraph. The paragraph's other sentences explain or tell *details* about the main idea.

EXAMPLE As a boy in England, Thomas Paine learned the skills that helped him take his place in American history. Paine grew up in the city of London in the 1700s. He enjoyed ice skating and other outdoor activities. He also enjoyed reading and writing and often sat for hours with his books or with pen and paper.

The first sentence tells that the *main idea* is Thomas Paine's boyhood and some of the skills he practiced as a boy. The other sentences give more details about Paine's boyhood and his skills.

DIRECTIONS Complete the sentence to give details about the main idea in the paragraph above.

1. As a boy, Thomas Paine lived in the city of _____.

2. He enjoyed outdoor activities such as _____.

3. Paine also enjoyed _____ and _____.

DIRECTIONS Read the paragraph. Then circle the letter of the answer or answers that complete the sentences below.

While he was still living in London, Paine met Benjamin Franklin. Franklin urged Paine to go back with him to the American colonies. Here Paine began to write about England's unfair treatment of the colonies. He wrote a pamphlet called *Common Sense,* which was a powerful argument for American independence. Not everyone believed in the ideas set forth in *Common Sense.* Some colonists remained loyal to the King of England. These people, called "loyalists," thought *Common Sense* was an act of treason or betrayal. Most colonists, however, agreed with Paine's ideas. The pamphlet, *Common Sense,* helped spread the idea of independence and also caused Paine to be known as a respected writer.

1. The main idea of the paragraph is
   a. How Paine met Benjamin Franklin
   b. The pamphlet, *Common Sense*
   c. The loyalists
   d. Acts of treason

2. *Three* details in the paragraph are:
   a. Paine met Benjamin Franklin in London.
   b. *Common Sense* was a pamphlet arguing for loyalty to the king.
   c. Americans who remained loyal to the King were called "loyalists."
   d. *Common Sense* helped spread the idea of American independence.
   e. Franklin urged Paine to leave the colonies and go to England.

Read about Thomas Paine's contributions in his lifetime.

A. Thomas Jefferson and other patriots were asked to write a document to be sent to the King of England. This document stated that the colonies had the right to be independent. Jefferson often asked the advice of the respected writer, Thomas Paine, in drafting the document which became known as the Declaration of Independence.

B. When the Revolutionary War began, Paine enlisted in the Continental Army. As the war grew longer, many of the soldiers became discouraged. George Washington asked Paine to write words of encouragement to the soldiers. Paine reminded the men of their goal of freedom in a series of pamphlets called *The Crisis*.

C. After America won its war for independence, Paine returned to England. He wrote a book called *The Rights of Man* which strongly supported the French Revolution. While it made Paine a hero with many Frenchmen, it caused him to be exiled from England. He then went to France, where he got caught up in the revolution and put into prison.

D. Paine was eventually released from prison and allowed to return to the United States. Here he finished another work called *The Age of Reason*, which he had begun in prison. This book was very unpopular with most Americans. Although Paine was unwelcome at most social gatherings, President Thomas Jefferson remained his friend.

E. The contributions Thomas Paine made to America in its struggle for freedom were not honored during his lifetime. In 1945, however, Paine was elected to the Hall of Fame. He is recognized today as one of America's great patriots.

Answer the questions about some main ideas and details from the article you just read.

1. What is the main idea of paragraph A?

   _____

   _____

   _____

2. What was the name of the document that Jefferson and others were asked to write?

   _____

   _____

3. Why did Jefferson ask for Paine's help in writing the document?

   _____

   _____

4. What is the main idea of paragraph B?

   _____

   _____

5. Who asked Paine to write to the soldiers?

   _____

6. What was the series of pamphlets called?

   _____

7. What is the main idea of paragraph C?

   _____

   _____

8. What was the name of the book that caused Paine to be so unpopular after he returned to the United States?

   _____

9. What was the topic of *The Rights of Man?*

   _____

   _____

   _____

10. Who continued to be Paine's friend?

    _____

    _____

11. What honor was given to Paine after his death?

    _____

    _____

12. How is Paine thought of today?

    _____

    _____

REMEMBER Details explain a main idea.

Creatures of the Sea

Why do some sea animals have shells? What sea animals can spray "ink" to protect themselves? In this lesson, you'll read about some creatures of the sea as you learn about main ideas and details.

 ## KEYS to Main Idea and Details

Details tell more about a main idea.

LEARN The *main idea* of a paragraph tells what the whole paragraph is about. A main idea is often stated in the first sentence of a paragraph, although it may occur elsewhere in the paragraph. *Details* give more information about the main idea.

EXAMPLE Some scientists spend their lives studying whales, fish, turtles, and other forms of sea life. They have studied many underwater animals to discover some important facts about sea creatures.

Sea creatures, the main idea of the paragraph, is stated in the last sentence of the paragraph. The rest of the words in the paragraph give details about sea creatures.

DIRECTIONS Read the paragraph. Then write two details that tell more about the underlined main idea.

Creatures of the sea exist in a relatively constant or unchanging climate. Below eight hundred feet, the temperature of water does not vary more than five degrees.

1. _____

2. _____

DIRECTIONS Read the paragraph. Answer the questions by circling the letter of the correct answer or answers.

Creatures of the ocean can be large or small. The whale is the largest animal in the ocean. A whale can weigh up to fourteen thousand pounds when it is born. Some of the large game fish, like the swordfish, sailfish, and blue marlin are ten to twelve feet long. Many ocean fish are small enough to keep in an aquarium. Seahorses only grow to be about five inches tall. The hatchet fish and deep-sea angler are only three to three and one-half inches long. The smallest animals in the ocean cannot be seen without a microscope.

1. Which one idea best tells the main idea of the paragraph?
   a. Seahorses grow to be about five inches tall.
   b. Small sea creatures cannot be seen without a microscope.
   c. The whale is the largest ocean animal.
   d. There are large and small animals in the ocean.

2. Which three ideas tell details about the main idea?
   a. Newborn whales can weigh up to fourteen thousand pounds.
   b. Seahorses grow to be five feet tall.
   c. There are large and small animals in the ocean.
   d. Small sea creatures cannot be seen without a microscope.
   e. A microscope is fun to use.
   f. Many ocean fish are small enough to fit in an aquarium.

Read and Apply

DIRECTIONS Think about the main idea and the details that support the main idea as you read the three paragraphs about sea creatures. Underline the main idea sentence in each paragraph.

A. The smallest sea creatures eat tiny plants that float on the surface of the water. These plants are so small it would take thousands of them to fill one teaspoon. Without these tiny plants, no animals could live in the ocean. That is because the large sea animals depend upon smaller ones for their food. Small sea animals eat still smaller ones. This concept is called the food chain.

B. Each species of sea animals has its own way of defending itself or attacking its prey. Tunas, sharks, and barracudas have sharp teeth. They are also strong and fast. Snails, clams, and oysters move slowly. They protect themselves by withdrawing into their shells. The squid, the octopus, and some shrimp hide themselves from their enemies by spraying dark "ink" into the water around them. Some eels give electric shocks. Jellyfish and stingrays have poisoned spines.

C. Other forms of defense include coloring and shape. Many sea creatures are very colorful. They use their color to hide from their predators. Flatfish, rockfish, and pipefish all live among the grasses and seaweed. They are shaped and colored so it is very hard to see them among the blades of grass. They use the grass for protection. They also use it to conceal themselves from the small creatures they need for food.

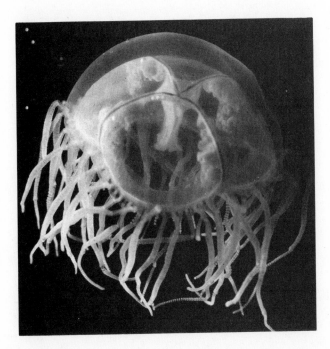

Write three details about each main idea from the article you just read.

A. Detail 1: _____

_____

_____   Detail 3: _____

_____

Detail 2: _____   _____

_____   _____

_____   **C.** Detail 1: _____

Detail 3: _____   _____

_____   _____

_____   Detail 2: _____

_____   _____

B. Detail 1: _____   _____

_____   Detail 3: _____

_____   _____

_____   _____

Detail 2: _____   _____

_____

DIRECTIONS Write *detail* or *main idea* before each statement.

_____   **1.** Clams and oysters move slowly.

_____   **2.** A food chain is how all animals exist.

_____   **3.** Each kind of sea creature has a method of defense.

_____   **4.** Large and small animals live together in the sea.

REMEMBER Learn more about the main idea by reading the details.

Red Cloud

If a group of people came into your area and forced you to change your entire way of living, would you try to fight or try to work out an agreement with them? In this lesson, you will read about a Sioux Indian who tried both methods as you learn about main ideas and details.

 ## 1 KEYS to Main Idea and Details

Details help explain a main idea.

LEARN The *main idea,* or topic, of a paragraph may be expressed in a sentence anywhere in the paragraph, or it may be suggested by a word or phrase. *Details* give more information about a main idea.

EXAMPLE In the 1800s, a ten-year-old boy named Red Cloud, chose his own pony. His tribe, the Sioux, expected him to tame the colt himself. Once he did so, Red Cloud could join the men of the tribe in their buffalo hunts.

The main idea, *the youth of Red Cloud,* is suggested by all the sentences that tell details about Red Cloud as a boy.

DIRECTIONS Read the paragraph. Then circle the number of the main idea sentence below.

Red Cloud listened to the older men telling stories about Sioux ceremonies and traditions. He learned to make paints from berries and plants, and how to make pictures with those paints. He learned to make his own weapons, and he improved his hunting skills.

1. Red Cloud made weapons to go hunting.
2. Red Cloud learned about his people and their ways.
3. Red Cloud listened to stories.

DIRECTIONS Read each paragraph. Then read each sentence below it and write *MI* before the *main idea* and *D* before each *detail*.

When Red Cloud was a young man, armies of soldiers came west to build forts in the Dakota territory. They also wanted to open up new routes through the territory. The Indians and soldiers met at Fort Laramie to work out an agreement. Red Cloud went with the other members of his tribe.

_____ 1. Armies of soldiers caused changes in the Dakota territory.

_____ 2. Red Cloud joined his people to keep peace.

_____ 3. An agreement was reached at Fort Laramie.

_____ 4. The soldiers wanted to open new routes.

When families began traveling through the Dakota territory by the wagonload, trouble brewed again. Many families settled in the area. Herds of buffalo were scared away or killed. Since buffalo was the main source of meat for Native Americans, they saw that their way of living was changing.

_____ 1. The buffalo was a food source for the Indians.

_____ 2. Wagons of people were moving onto the land.

_____ 3. Buffalo were scared away or killed.

_____ 4. Problems remained between the Indians and the settlers.

Read and Apply

DIRECTIONS Look for the main idea and some details in each paragraph as you read more about Red Cloud.

A. Red Cloud, now a leader of his tribe, felt that all the tribes must band together. He organized raids to attack a fort the soldiers were building. Captain Fetterman, the leader of the fort, bragged that his men could easily defeat the Sioux nation. Red Cloud and his men decided to ambush the soldiers. There was a bloody battle, which Red Cloud and his men won. The surviving soldiers withdrew from the burning fort. The Indians hoped they could now live in peace.

B. By now Red Cloud was greatly respected by both the Indians and the settlers. The soldiers asked him to sign a peace treaty promising that more Indian land would not be taken away. The treaty was soon broken, and many Indians were forced to move onto reservations, areas of land where Indians were given food and shelter by the United States government.

C. Since the Indians didn't want to live on reservations, Red Cloud made frequent trips to Washington, D.C. and other eastern cities in search of peace. He also spread the message that Indians wanted to live on their own lands as their forefathers had done.

D. Some Indians felt that Red Cloud had betrayed them. They felt he should still be fighting the settlers instead of trying to make peace with them. When Red Cloud was about sixty years old, his tribe took away his chief status. Red Cloud lived on a reservation in South Dakota until he died at the age of eighty-seven. As an old man, he taught the younger Indians about the Sioux customs and traditions.

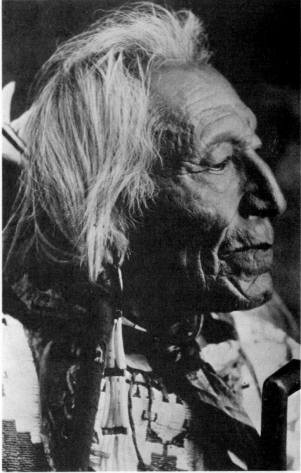

DIRECTIONS Four of the sentences are main ideas from the paragraphs you just read. The other sentences are details. Write the letter of its correct paragraph before each of the four main ideas.

_____ **1.** Red Cloud was no longer respected by all his tribesmen.

_____ **2.** Red Cloud led warriors in battles for Indian rights.

_____ **3.** Red Cloud was asked to sign a treaty.

_____ **4.** Red Cloud sought peace in Washington and other cities.

_____ **5.** Red Cloud was respected as a spokesman for peace.

_____ **6.** Red Cloud told the soldiers that his people wanted their land.

DIRECTIONS Write each of the main idea sentences from above in order. Write *two* details from the article to support each main idea.

A. Main Idea: _____

Detail: _____

Detail: _____

B. Main Idea: _____

Detail: _____

Detail: _____

C. Main Idea: _____

Detail: _____

Detail: _____

D. Main Idea: _____

Detail: _____

Detail: _____

REMEMBER Finding the main idea and details helps you read for meaning.

Making Chocolate Candy Bars

Have you ever wondered how chocolate candy bars are made? In this lesson, you'll read about the production of chocolate candy bars as you learn about the order, or sequence, in which things happen.

 KEYS to Sequence

Sequence is the order in which things happen.

LEARN Things that happen are called events. Events happen in a certain order. The order of events is called the *sequence of events*. If events are out of order, a story doesn't make sense. Some words are clues to a sequence.

EXAMPLE First, I bought a candy bar. Then I put it in my jeans pocket. After my game in the hot sun, I found a melted mess.

The word *first* is a clue to the beginning of the events. The word *then* is a clue to the middle event, and *after* gives a clue to the ending event.

DIRECTIONS Read each word or phrase. Write *F* on the line before a word or phrase that gives a clue to what happened first. Write *M* for middle or *E* for a clue word or phrase of an ending event.

_____ first

_____ then

_____ near the end

_____ in the beginning

_____ at last

_____ before

_____ following

_____ later

_____ next

_____ finally

_____ after

_____ last

Practice With Sequence

Read the paragraph. Then read each group of sentences below. Number each group of sentences to show their correct sequence.

The most important ingredient in chocolate is the cocoa bean. Cocoa beans grow in shells, or pods, on trees in Africa and South America. The first step in harvesting the beans is to cut the pods from the trees with long knives. Then the pods are cut open and the beans are removed. At first, cocoa beans are white. They are left out in the sun to dry. After a few days, they turn brown from exposure to air. Next, they're sent by ship to countries all over the world. Finally, the beans are carried on trains and trucks to factories, where they are used to make chocolate.

A. _____ Workers cut the bean pods from the trees.

_____ Cocoa beans grow in pods on trees.

_____ The pods are cut open.

B. _____ Air turns the beans brown.

_____ The white beans are left out in the sun.

_____ The beans are removed from the pods.

C. _____ The beans are sent by ship to many countries.

_____ The beans are left in the sun to dry out.

_____ Trains and trucks carry the beans to candy factories.

Read and Apply

DIRECTIONS Read each paragraph and the sentences below it. Number the sentences to show their correct sequence.

A. After the cocoa beans arrive at the candy factory, they are roasted in very hot air. Then they are put into machines that break them up and remove their shells. Only the soft center, or nib, of the bean is left. Next, the nibs are crushed into a creamy liquid, called butter. This butter is what makes chocolate smooth.

_____ The nibs are crushed into butter.

_____ The beans are put into machines that remove their shells.

_____ The beans are roasted in very hot air.

B. To make milk chocolate, milk must be cooked until much of its water has boiled away. Then sugar is added, and the mixture becomes thick and sticky. This milk mixture is then combined with the chocolate mixture. Next, the milk chocolate is poured into a huge stone tub where stone rollers rub it against the sides of the tub. After three days of rubbing, the milk chocolate is finally smooth enough to make candy bars.

_____ The milk mixture is combined with the chocolate mixture.

_____ Milk is cooked and sweetened until it is thick and sticky.

_____ Stone rollers rub the milk chocolate for three days.

_____ The milk chocolate is smooth enough to make candy bars.

The smooth milk chocolate is now poured into a machine that hangs above a moving belt. On the belt are metal molds shaped like candy bars. The machine fills each mold with chocolate. Next, the chocolate-filled molds take a bumpy ride through a cooling tunnel. The shaking of the belt levels out the chocolate and gets rid of any air bubbles. The cooling tunnel hardens the chocolate. After the candy bars come out of the tunnel, they are removed from the molds. Then each one is inspected, and imperfect bars are pulled out of the line. The perfect bars are then wrapped by another machine and finally packed into boxes for shipment to stores.

1. **a.** A belt takes the chocolate-filled molds through a cooling tunnel.
   b. The milk chocolate is poured into a machine.
   c. The machine pours chocolate into molds on a moving belt.

   The best sequence is:

   a, b, c   c, b, a

   b, a, c   b, c, a

2. **a.** Smooth and hardened candy bars come out of a tunnel.
   b. The candy bars are wrapped, packed into boxes, and shipped to stores.
   c. Each candy bar is inspected to make sure it is perfect.
   d. The candy bars are removed from the molds.

   The best sequence is:

   a, b, c, d   a, d, c, b

   d, c, b, a   c, d, a, b

REMEMBER Some words are clues to the correct sequence of events.

Camera Capers

Taking pictures of wild animals is not an easy job. In this lesson, you'll learn about the order in which things happen as you read about some funny things that animals do when people try to photograph them.

KEYS to Sequence

The sequence of events is the order in which things happen.

LEARN   The order in which things happen is called the *sequence*. Knowing the sequence helps you make sense of a story. Clue words like *first* or *at the start* help you know which event happened first. Words like *then, next,* or *later* are clues to middle events, while *finally* and *last* are ending clues.

EXAMPLE   We purchased the film next. At last, we were ready to go. We decided in the beginning to get more film.

The events do not make sense because they are out of order. The words *in the beginning* tell that the decision to get more film happened first.

DIRECTIONS   Write the above paragraph so that its sentences are in an order that makes sense.

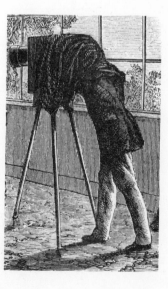

_____

_____

_____

_____

2 Practice With Sequence

DIRECTIONS Read each paragraph and the pairs of sentences below it. Mark an X before the sentence in each pair that tells what happened first.

A. A monkey appeared right in front of the tour bus just after it had parked. The monkey seemed to be begging to have his picture taken. After the passengers and cameras left the bus, the monkey scampered inside. The photographers then peered in the windows to see the monkey enjoying a stolen snack of crackers.

1. _____ **a.** The bus stopped and parked.

   _____ **b.** The monkey appeared in front of the bus.

2. _____ **a.** The monkey had a stolen snack of crackers.

   _____ **b.** The monkey ran into the empty bus.

B. Just before Tom fell asleep after a long day's work, a mouse chose to explore the tent. Tom slapped the ground to chase the mouse away. Later, however, a slap on the ground failed to scare off an animal of another kind. A whiff of a peculiar odor suggested that a skunk was paying a visit! Tom lay very still until, finally, the skunk wandered off.

3. _____ **a.** He slapped the ground to chase another animal away.

   _____ **b.** He slapped the ground to chase the mouse away.

4. _____ **a.** The skunk moved on.

   _____ **b.** A very bad odor told Tom a skunk was near.

Read and Apply

DIRECTIONS Read about some attempts to photograph water animals in their natural surroundings.

When Chris dove under water, she saw just what she wanted to capture on film. Some sea lions were swimming about. Chris positioned herself nearby, but just then a sea lion swam swiftly toward her. It started to bump and push Chris as she tried to take its picture. Another sea lion then swam forward and grabbed the wire that connected the flashbulb to Chris' camera.

Chris chased the sea lions around and around because she needed the flash to take pictures in the dark water. Finally, she retrieved the wire but, by this time, she was laughing so hard she could hardly hold the camera.

Tim, on the other hand, decided to take some pictures of a group of muskrats that made their home in a pond. To get near their home, he made a small raft. Then he covered the raft with weeds to help hide himself as he drew near.

As Tim floated close to the muskrats, they seemed to sense his presence and jumped into the water. Before Tim knew what was happening, a muskrat had climbed onto the raft and was eying Tim closely. Then, it crawled even closer. The next thing Tim knew, it had crawled up onto his back.

Before many minutes passed, the raft was full of muskrats, and there was Tim, surrounded by the wet, furry creatures. They now began to pile weeds from the pond onto the raft. Tim decided it was time to leave the scene, pictures or no pictures.

Read each group of sentences about the story you just read. Number the sentences to show the correct sequence.

1. _____ Chris was laughing too hard to take pictures.

   _____ A sea lion grabbed the wire that Chris had to have.

   _____ A sea lion started bumping and pushing Chris.

2. _____ The muskrats started to pile pond weeds on top of the raft.

   _____ Tim wanted to take pictures of muskrats in their home.

   _____ The muskrats climbed on Tim's raft.

DIRECTIONS Read the paragraph. Then read the sentences below and write the letters in order on the lines to tell the best sentence sequence.

First, Rollie and his friend arranged their tripod on the ground below the tree. Then they set the camera on the tripod before they climbed the tree to watch for bears. Along came a wild wolf, who sniffed the tripod and camera before running off with it. Rollie yelled, and the wolf instantly stopped and dropped the equipment. As Rollie jumped down, though, the wolf grabbed its prize and ran off again.

Then the fellows made a plan. Rollie lay in the grass and made noises like a young animal. When the wolf let go of the equipment and started over to check out the sounds, Rollie's friend grabbed the tripod and camera and made off, with Rollie close behind.

1. a. The wolf ran off with the tripod and camera.

   b. The wolf sniffed the equipment.

   c. The wolf let go of the equipment to check out some sounds.

   The best order is:

   _____ _____ _____

2. a. Rollie made noises like a young animal.

   b. The wolf dropped the equipment.

   c. Rollie's friend grabbed the equipment.

   The best order is:

   _____ _____ _____

REMEMBER Look for clue words to place events in order.

Be Aware!

Think about all the knowledge that is stored in your brain. In this lesson, you will learn to be aware of and to use your "knowledge bank." You'll also read about something you'll want to avoid.

 ## 1 KEYS to Making Predictions

Predictions are guesses that are based on good information.

LEARN   Before you read and as you read, your "knowledge bank" helps you predict what will come next. Making predictions, or good guesses, helps you get more meaning from your reading.

EXAMPLE   Read the poem. Do you know what the poem is about?

Your knowledge of the meaning of the word *Beware* helps you predict that the article you'll read is about something dangerous.

> Beware!
>
> See leaflets three?
> Just let it be!
> See berries white?
> Just flee the site!

DIRECTIONS Use the above verse to answer the questions.

1. What topic do you think the article will be about? _____

_____

2. What word clues helped you make this prediction? _____

_____

3. What information in your "knowledge bank" helped you

   make this prediction? _____

2 Practice Making Predictions

DIRECTIONS Suppose you wanted to make a costume to wear to a party. You would begin by deciding how you want to look. Next, you plan the costume. Your thinking and planning are important steps in creating a good costume. Doing a good job of reading is something like making a costume. Making predictions, or thinking and planning before you read, gets you ready to gather and remember the most important ideas.

Write the name of an animal. Then use your "knowledge bank" to complete the information about that animal.

1. Animal _____
   _____

2. How the animal looks: _____
   _____

3. What the animal eats: _____
   _____

4. Things the animal does: _____
   _____

5. Places the animal lives: _____
   _____

6. List five important words an author might use in a story or article about this animal. Do not use words like *is, and,* or *the.*

   _____

   _____

   _____

   _____

7. You've just made some predictions about what you think you'll find written about this animal. Now find a book or article on the animal. As you read, circle each word or idea in your predictions that the author uses. Think about how much you already knew about this animal. Your "knowledge bank" guided you in searching for some important ideas. You also added some new ideas to your "knowledge bank." They will help you make predictions the next time you read something about this animal.

DIRECTIONS Reread the verse on the first page of this lesson and then read the following article.

Ignoring the warning in the little rhyme on page 93 can take the enjoyment out of your outdoor fun. Avoiding ivy poisoning is much simpler than curing it. It is wise to bring a little awareness along with you on your next outdoor picnic or hike.

Nearly everyone who touches poison ivy ends up with miserable itching and blisters. Unfortunately there is no cure except to ease the itching with creams and lotions and wait for the discomfort to disappear on its own.

Poison ivy, like other ivy plants, grows in many places. It can be seen climbing walls, fences, and trees or lying hidden in the grass. It might also show itself as an upright bush.

Poison ivy can be difficult to identify since its leaves vary in size, color and shape, depending on the amount of sunlight it gets. A good sign, however, is a plant with three leaves along with berry-like fruits that are white and waxy. The berries often stay on the vine all winter. Though poison ivy plants are pretty with their red leaf buds in spring, green leaves in summer and multi-colored hues in fall, it is wise to stay clear of them at all times of the year.

The vines of poison ivy are troublesome to dispose of. Burning the plants only carries the poison into the air. Using tools with gloved hands only spreads the poison to all that it touches. If you use the tools or clothes later, it could spell trouble.

If you ever think you may have been around poison ivy, scrub promptly with soap followed by several clear water rinses. Similarly treat your dog or other pet as they can carry the poison on their fur.

Better yet, be aware and beware! Learn to recognize poison ivy and stay clear of any suspicious-looking plants.

DIRECTIONS Look back at the predictions you made on the first page of this lesson. Check your predictions by answering the questions:

1. Did you guess the story would be about a poisonous plant?

   _____

2. Underline any sentence in the above article that is about ideas you predicted would be included.

DIRECTIONS Use your "knowledge bank" along with clues from the titles of the books to write predictions about the content of each book.

1. *Cranberry Thanksgiving* by Wende and Harry Devlin

   _____

   _____

   _____

2. *The Digger Wasp* by George Mendoza

   _____

   _____

   _____

3. *Matt's Mitt* by Marilyn Sachs

   _____

   _____

   _____

4. *Corn is Maize—The Gift of the Indians* by Aliki

   _____

   _____

   _____

It can be difficult to make good predictions about a topic you know little or nothing about. In this case, you need to stop and gather more information. You can do this by:

1. Asking questions of others about the topic.

2. Reading an easier book with pictures about the topic.

3. Viewing a video, film, or other material on the topic.

REMEMBER Think, read, predict, and read some more.

Jokes and Riddles

Rib-tickling jokes and puzzling riddles are fun to read. In this lesson, you'll practice doing the special thinking that allows you to "get" jokes and solve riddles. You'll probably laugh a little, too!

KEYS to Making Inferences

Your own ideas + words you read = inference

LEARN You make an *inference* by combining your own ideas with the words you read. Inferences help you understand what you read.

EXAMPLE Tim: What's the tallest building in the world?
Matt: I haven't the slightest idea. What?
Tim: The library. It has the most stories.

To "get" the punch line to Tim's joke, you made an inference. You read the words, or "on-the-page" clues, and used "in-the-head" clues as you thought about "tall buildings," "libraries," and "stories." What two meanings did you think about for the word *stories*?

1. _____   2. _____

DIRECTIONS Read the joke. Write the clues you used to understand the joke.
Why is a baseball game like a stack of pancakes?
They both depend on the batter!

1. Word clues: _____

2. Own ideas: _____

_____

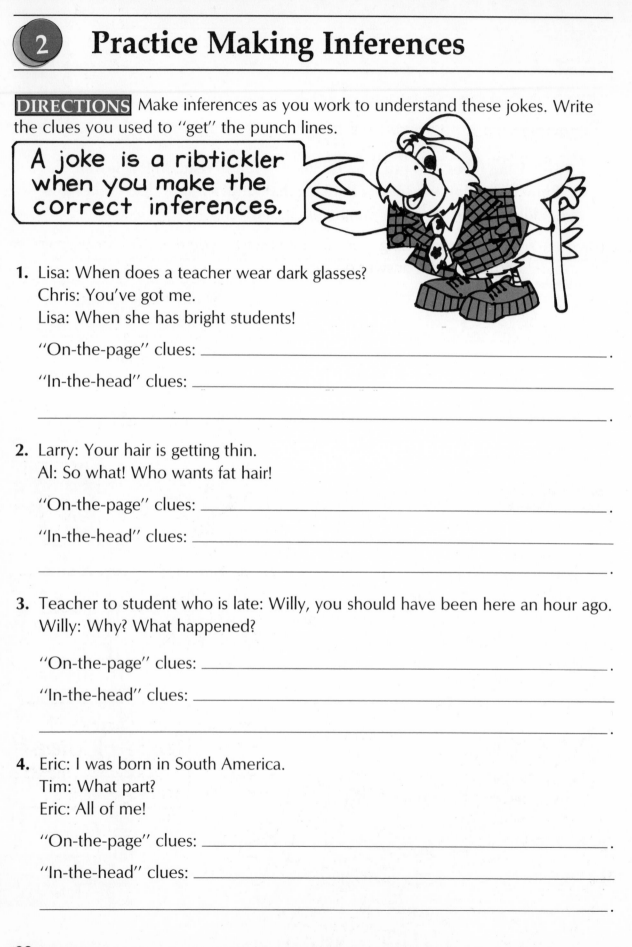

2 Practice Making Inferences

DIRECTIONS Make inferences as you work to understand these jokes. Write the clues you used to "get" the punch lines.

> A joke is a ribtickler when you make the correct inferences.

1. Lisa: When does a teacher wear dark glasses?
   Chris: You've got me.
   Lisa: When she has bright students!

   "On-the-page" clues: _____.

   "In-the-head" clues: _____

   _____.

2. Larry: Your hair is getting thin.
   Al: So what! Who wants fat hair!

   "On-the-page" clues: _____.

   "In-the-head" clues: _____

   _____.

3. Teacher to student who is late: Willy, you should have been here an hour ago.
   Willy: Why? What happened?

   "On-the-page" clues: _____.

   "In-the-head" clues: _____

   _____.

4. Eric: I was born in South America.
   Tim: What part?
   Eric: All of me!

   "On-the-page" clues: _____.

   "In-the-head" clues: _____

   _____.

98 Making Inferences

3 Read and Apply

DIRECTIONS In a "Hink-Pink" riddle, the answer is made up of two words that rhyme. Each word has one syllable.

What do you call a witch's purse? *(hag bag)*

A "Hinky-Pinky" riddle has two syllables in each word of its rhyming answer.

What would you ask for if you needed a larger shovel? *(bigger digger)*

Solve the riddles by combining clues from the words you read with clues from your own head. Write the answer on the line.

Hink-Pink Riddles

1. What do sheep use to tell time?

   _____

2. What do you call a hobo caught in a thunderstorm?

   _____

3. What do you call a puppy's diary?

   _____

4. What kind of sound does a dog make at night?

   _____

Hinky-Pinky Riddles

1. What's a good name for a talkative parrot?

   _____

2. What would you call a skinny young horse?

   _____

3. What could you call a bunny's daily routine?

   _____

4. What is shot from a thin bow?

   _____

How about some riddles? Ready to make inferences?

DIRECTIONS Read the cartoons. Answer the questions.

DENNIS THE MENACE

"I HOPE YOU DON'T GET TOO LONESOME, MR. WILSON..MY MOM SAYS I CAN'T COME OVER 'TIL THE BLIZZARD STOPS."

"But Mommy, I can't be in the same boat with Nicky. His boat just sank!"

1. Who made the telephone call?

What makes you think this?

2. Will Mr. Wilson be lonely for Dennis?

What makes you think this?

3. Does Dennis think Mr. Wilson misses him?

What makes you think this?

4. About how old is the girl?

What clues led you to this answer?

5. What does "in the same boat" mean to you?

What do the words mean to the girl?

6. How does the boy feel?

What makes you think so?

REMEMBER Use book clues plus head clues to make inferences.

Grapes To Raisins

In this lesson, you will practice combining what you already know with what you read. You'll also learn how grapes become raisins.

1 KEYS to Making Inferences

When you add your knowledge to what you read, you make inferences.

LEARN   When you fill in your own ideas as you read, you are making *inferences*. When you read a recipe that calls for an egg, you make an inference. You use your knowledge that *egg* means only the egg white and yolk not the shell.

DIRECTIONS Read the paragraph and complete the statements.

Raisins are a dried fruit made from different kinds of grapes. Small sweet grapes without seeds make seedless raisins, but not all raisins are seedless.

1. Grapes are in the food group called _____. I know this because

    the paragraph tells me that _____.

2. Some grapes have _____ in them. I know this because the

    paragraph tells me that _____

    _____.

3. Grapes must be _____ to become raisins. I know this because

    the paragraph tells me that _____

    _____.

DIRECTIONS Read the paragraphs. Then answer the questions below.

Thanks to a group of priests, the California raisin industry was started in the state's central valleys. Grape vines were planted around the missions to help supply food for the hungry.

Today, most California raisins are grown from seedless green grapes which have thin skins that dry easily in the sun. Grapes need hot weather and a good supply of water. A spring frost, strong winds, or hail can damage the buds or bruise the grapes and spoil the crop. Mild California weather is usually perfect for growing grapes.

1. Why would you be likely to find more grape farmers in California than in states like Wisconsin, or Minnesota?

_____

_____

_____

My best "on-the-page" clues were:

_____

_____

_____

My best "in-the-head" clues were:

_____

_____

2. Why might a California grape grower have a bad season?

_____

_____

_____

My best "on-the-page" clues were:

_____

_____

_____

My best "in-the-head" clues were:

_____

_____

Read and Apply

DIRECTIONS Read the article and answer the questions on page 104.

During a good growing season, grapes are ready for harvest in August. They must be carefully handled to avoid being bruised. The grape pickers use a curved knife to pick the clusters quickly by hand. Workers are careful not to miss any clusters of grapes, since it takes over four pounds of grapes to produce just one pound of raisins.

As the grapes are cut, workers spread them out between the rows of vines on large sheets of clean brown paper. Often one side of the paper will be plastic coated to keep ground moisture from seeping through to the drying grapes.

The grapes are left to dry outdoors for the next ten to fifteen days. Farmers hope the weather during this time will be dry and warm but not too sunny. Too much rain can spoil the crop, and too much sunshine can cause the drying grapes to shrink and darken from lack of moisture.

After drying, the grapes on the sheets of paper are rolled into bundles. Workers leave the bundles in the sun for another week. The bundles are then unrolled, and the raisins are put through a sifting machine. A screen in the sifting machine separates the raisins from sand and leaf particles.

The clean raisins are now put into great wooden bins, called sweat boxes. Here the raisins absorb moisture from one another. When the raisins are equally plump and juicy, they're sent to the packing house.

In the packing house, stems are removed from the raisins by machines. Then they are sorted, washed, inspected, and pressed into boxes for people to enjoy as a quick energy snack.

Read each statement. Circle *T* for true or *F* for false.

1. Plastic-coated paper is used to prevent too much moisture.   T   F

2. If it is too sunny during drying time, a grape harvest is not affected.   T   F

3. Workers look for imperfect raisins before they are boxed.   T   F

4. If the growing season is not good, a harvest in August is impossible.   T   F

5. Dark grapes are caused by lack of moisture.   T   F

6. All raisins are the same size when they're put into the sweat boxes.   T   F

7. A one-pound box of raisins was once more than four pounds of grapes.   T   F

DIRECTIONS Read each paragraph and the statements below it. Circle the word in parentheses that completes each statement.

1. Raisins are grapes that have lost more than three-fourths of their original moisture in a process called dehydration. You can watch dehydration at home by placing a few grapes on a sunny window sill for several days.

   A. A raisin weighs (less/more) than a grape.

   B. Dehydration is a process of (gaining/losing) moisture.

   C. Raisins have less than (three-fourths/one-fourth) of the moisture of the original grapes.

2. Once grapes have ripened, they must be quickly picked from their vines. Workers must be ready to work fast, since a whole harvest could be lost if the grapes get overly ripe.

   A. Ripe grapes are picked quickly to prevent too much (ripening/picking).

   B. There is (much/little) time to waste once the grapes are ripe.

REMEMBER Inferences = your own ideas + words on the page

Bedtime Stories

Some animals snooze in weird ways and places. In this lesson, you will read about some unusual animal sleeping arrangements. You'll also learn to tell the difference between fact statements and those that tell what someone thinks.

1 KEYS to Facts and Opinions

A fact can be checked, while an opinion tells how someone feels.

LEARN   A *fact* tells something about a person, place, or thing. Facts can be checked to see whether they are true or false.

Some bees sleep in groups to keep warm.

An *opinion* tells what someone thinks. We cannot prove that opinions are right or wrong. People can have different opinions about the same thing.

Betsy thinks it's fun to watch bees gather honey from flowers.

DIRECTIONS Read each sentence. Circle the word to tell if the sentence states a fact or an opinion.

1. Katie's cat sleeps at the foot of her bed.   fact   opinion
2. My horses like to sleep in the barn.   fact   opinion
3. It's not a good idea to disturb a sleep-ing bear.   fact   opinion
4. Many animals don't sleep at night.   fact   opinion
5. Cows can sleep when they are standing up.   fact   opinion

Fact and Opinion **105**

Practice With Fact and Opinion

DIRECTIONS Deciding whether a statement is a fact or an opinion is easy if you do one or both of these things:

- Ask yourself if it can be proven. If so, it's a fact.

- Ask yourself if someone else could feel differently about it. If so, it's an opinion.

Read each sentence. If the sentence is a fact, tell why. If the sentence is an opinion, tell how someone else might feel differently.

1. Animals are fascinating creatures.

_____

_____

_____

2. A snake's body is as cold or warm as the air around it.

_____

_____

_____

3. Cats sleep for short periods of time.

_____

_____

_____

4. Dogs are truly man's best friend.

_____

_____

_____

DIRECTIONS Read the fact and opinion that Jody wrote about herself. Then think about yourself. Write a sentence telling a fact about yourself. Write a sentence to tell an opinion of yours.

Jody's fact: I take horse riding lessons.

Jody's opinion: There is nothing better than a horse.

My fact: _____

_____

My opinion: _____

_____

Read and Apply

DIRECTIONS Some animals sleep in or near a waterbed every night. Read the stories. Underline the sentences that are facts. Then write on the lines the two sentences that state opinions.

1. Hermit crabs seem to play musical chairs. They find snail shells to sleep in and return to them night after night. Hermit crabs must feel right at home in a snail's shell. When they outgrow their old shells, they leave them for younger crabs and go off in search of larger sleeping quarters.

   A. _Hermit crabs must feel right at home in a snails shell._

   B. _Hermit crabs seem to play musical chairs._

2. A brown seal is another animal that sleeps in a waterbed. It probably doesn't worry about outgrowing it. This kind of seal goes to sleep and sinks to the ocean floor. Holding its breath, it rests there for several minutes. Then it acts

   just like a sleepwalker. It rises in its sleep to take some breaths of air. Still asleep, it sinks again.

   A. _Just like a sleepwalker_

   B. _Still, asleep, it sincks again._

3. Puffers form a funny-looking pile on the beach. They leave the deep water and go to the shallow water of the beach when it's time to sleep. They must think the beach is very tiny. Two or three puffers pile up on top of each other. They throw sand over their backs to keep warm.

   A. _Puffers form a funny-looking pile on the beach._
   waterbel

   B. _It probhaly dosent wory about outgrawing it_

Tree branches provide a sleeping place for the orangutan. This ape wraps each long arm around a branch. There it swings as it holds on tightly. If an orangutan had a nightmare, it might fall out of bed! This could be a real disaster, since its bed is often as high as forty feet in the air.

Speaking of sleeping in trees, wild turkeys do just that. They choose the same tree each night, even if hunters are nearby. At bedtime, the turkeys run to their tree and circle it. They push and shove each other for awhile before settling down on the tree limbs. They act so silly—a lot like someone who's called a "real turkey."

One might also call a giraffe a "real turkey" since he often sleeps in a standing position. Giraffes' knee joints lock so they don't topple over as they stand there with their long necks hanging down. It's hard to believe that giraffes don't wake up with a stiff neck. Baby giraffes don't sleep like this, though. They lie down in a twisted-up position.

__T__ **1.** Wild turkeys sleep in the same place each night even if hunters are nearby.

__T__ **2.** Giraffes sleep in a standing position.

__T__ **3.** An orangutan that had a nightmare might fall out of bed.

__F__ **4.** Baby giraffes don't sleep like their parents who lock their knees while standing up to sleep.

__F__ **5.** Wild turkeys act so silly at bedtime.

__T__ **6.** An orangutan sleeps while holding on to tree branches.

__F__ **7.** Giraffes should wake up in the morning with stiff necks.

__T__ **8.** Wild turkeys push and shove each other at roosting time.

REMEMBER An opinion cannot be proven, but a fact can be.

Scraps Of The Past

Handsewn quilts were made in colonial days as warm covers for beds and as hangings to cover drafty openings. In this lesson, you'll read about the lasting use of this old style of needlework. You'll also learn to tell the difference between facts and opinions.

1 KEYS to Facts and Opinions

Facts can be checked, while opinions cannot be proven.

LEARN A fact is a statement about a person, place, or thing that can be proven. It tells about something that is true.

Fact: Handsewn quilts are often used as artwork.

An opinion cannot be proven, since people have different feelings and beliefs. Words like *think, seem, thought, might, look like,* and *probably* give clues that statements are opinions.

Opinion: People think old quilts are lovely decorations.

DIRECTIONS Read each sentence. Write its number on the correct line below to tell if it is a fact or opinion.

1. Anna believes that the best quilts were made in Indiana.
2. Mary Ann was eight years old when she learned to quilt.
3. During hard times, people paid their debts with quilts.
4. Old quilts are probably better than new quilts.

Facts: _____ Opinions: _____

2 Practice With Fact and Opinion

DIRECTIONS Read each sentence about quilts. Identify each statement by writing *fact* or *opinion* on the line.

1. _____ Jill thought the blue and white quilt was the most beautiful quilt she had ever seen.

2. _____ There are many different quilt patterns.

3. _____ Some people believe that when you sleep under a quilt for the first time, your dreams come true.

4. _____ I don't like the striped quilt as much as the one with flowers on it.

5. _____ Quilts help keep you warm when you sleep.

6. _____ Many antique shops sell old quilts.

7. _____ My brother thinks old quilts are more interesting than new quilts.

8. _____ You'll probably never see a quilt that old again.

9. _____ Maggie's is surely the prettiest of the forty quilts entered in the contest.

10. _____ Grandmother told us a story about how she helped make quilts when she was a little girl.

11. _____ The patches on Jeff's quilt look like stars.

12. _____ Several women and their daughters would work together to produce a quilt in colonial times.

13. _____ People in colonial times used fabric scraps and pieces of old clothing to make quilts.

DIRECTIONS Look for facts and opinions as you read the story.

It was a rainy day at Grandmother's house. I thought I would be bored because there was nothing to do, until Grandmother had an idea. "Come with me to the attic and I'll show you some treasures," she said.

When she opened one of the old chests in the corner, I thought I was looking at a bunch of old blankets. When Grandmother unfolded them, however, I saw the prettiest quilts I had ever seen. There were quilts with flowers, quilts with stars, and even a quilt with pieces put together to look like old schoolhouses.

Grandmother had many stories to tell about the quilts. "Look at this one carefully," she said. "It's made from the cloth sacks that flour came in when I was a child. Purple and pink bags seemed to make the best flowers, so I saved them to use in this quilt. You'll probably never see materials with designs like these again," she laughed.

"Now look at this old star quilt. Why, I remember how my mama used to hang it over the window in our bedroom to keep out the draft. It was so cold in that room that I thought my sister and I would freeze to death before the winter was over! My mama believed there was nothing better than a big quilt to keep you cozy and warm."

My grandmother looked as though she were daydreaming now. "When summer came," she said softly, "we discovered that quilts could be used for all kinds of fun times. We used the red quilt to make a tent on the front porch. That tent seemed big enough to hold a circus."

"Sometimes," she went on, "we spread the yellow and white checked quilt out on the grass by the river for a picnic lunch. I don't think we ever went for a wagon ride without the green striped quilt to wrap up in when the sun went down. Look at this pretty piece. This was my sister's favorite. She liked the checkerboard pattern so much."

Grandmother ran her fingers over another quilt and then looked at me. "Well, Honey," she sighed. "There's probably a story behind this one, too, but I can't seem to remember it. I guess all my memories are just about as old as these quilts."

DIRECTIONS Write the number of each fact sentence on an open shape on the fact quilt. Write the number of each opinion sentence on an open shape on the opinion quilt.

1. I thought I would be bored.
2. It was a rainy day.
3. Grandmother took me to the attic.
4. The quilts were stacked neatly in the trunk.
5. At first, the quilts seemed like a bunch of old blankets.
6. I thought the quilts were the prettiest I'd ever seen.
7. Grandmother showed me her quilts.
8. Grandmother seemed to see me again.
9. Grandmother unfolded the quilts.
10. Purple and pink bags seemed to make the best flowers.
11. I thought my sister and I would freeze to death in the cold room.
12. Grandmother saved flour sacks so she could make them into quilts.
13. The red quilt tent seemed big enough for a circus.
14. Quilts are used for many things.
15. Mama hung the star quilt over the window.
16. We wrapped up in the green striped quilt.
17. Grandmother looked as though she were daydreaming.
18. The yellow and white checked quilt was our picnic quilt.

Fact Quilt

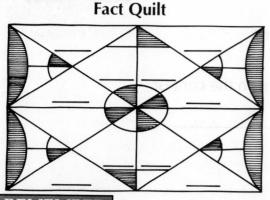

Opinion Quilt

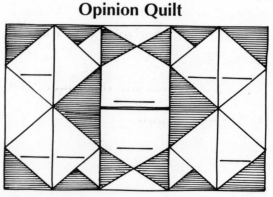

REMEMBER Facts can be proven, but opinions cannot.

How Earmuffs Were Invented

If your ears were always cold, would you think about inventing something to keep them warm? That's just what someone did many years ago. In this lesson, you will read about how earmuffs were invented. You'll also learn about cause and effect, or how some things cause other things to happen.

1 KEYS to Cause and Effect

When one thing happens, it can cause something else to happen.

LEARN When we think about *why* something happens, we are thinking about the *cause*. When we think about *what happened,* or the result of a cause, we are thinking about the *effect*.

EXAMPLE *What* happened? *Earmuffs were invented.* This is the *effect*.
Why did it happen? *Someone had cold ears.* This is the *cause*.

DIRECTIONS Read the sentences. Write the words that tell the effect after the question, "What happened?" Write the words that tell the cause after the question, "Why did it happen?"

1. Since Sarah was the best figure skater, she won the contest.

What happened? _____

Why did it happen? _____

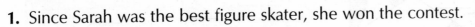

DIRECTIONS Read each sentence. Think about *what happens* to find the *effect*. Think about *why it happens* to find the *cause*. Circle the word that tells if the underlined part of the sentence is the *cause* or the *effect*.

1. Because it got so cold last night, the pond is frozen hard enough to skate on.

         cause   effect

2. School was closed today because we had a bad snowstorm last night.

         cause   effect

3. Winter is my favorite season since I like to ski and ice skate.

         cause   effect

4. Because it was so warm today, our snowman has melted.

         cause   effect

5. In the winter, you can tell when an animal has been in your yard because you can see its tracks in the snow.

         cause   effect

6. Tina can't see any of the grass in her yard since there is so much snow on the ground.

         cause   effect

7. Because it sticks together well, wet snow makes the best snowballs.

         cause   effect

8. Kenny's ears were cold, so he put his earmuffs on.

         cause   effect

DIRECTIONS Read about how a young boy solved a problem.

In December 1873, Chester Greenwood received a pair of ice skates for his fifteenth birthday. Although it was a blustery, cold winter day, Chester was anxious to try out his new skates at the local skating pond.

Chester tugged on his hat to pull it down over his ears before going outside. He knew, though, that shortly his hat would slide up until his ears were bare and cold. Then he'd have to go inside quickly to warm his ears so they would not become painfully frostbitten.

Within an hour, Chester began to feel his ears getting cold. He skated toward the shore. He didn't want to go in because he would miss all the skating fun. His friends would probably skate all day because their ears didn't seem to get cold as quickly as his did. He was angry about having to quit skating just because he couldn't keep his ears protected.

As usual, Chester's frustration became a challenge to him. He'd have to find a solution to his problem. What he needed was an ear protector! Because the idea sounded so simple to him, Chester couldn't believe no one had thought of it earlier.

Chester ran all the way home to ask his grandmother for help with his new idea. She was an expert at sewing and made many of the family's clothes. She happily gathered some scraps of fur and cloth for him while he grabbed a pair of pliers and set to work bending a piece of strong wire. Chester watched his grandmother as she carefully sewed the fabric onto his crude wire frame.

Chester put his ear protectors over his head and ears. He covered the wire with his knit cap and returned to the skating pond. His friends laughed because they thought the ear protectors looked ridiculous. They changed their minds, however, when they saw how much longer Chester was able to stay outside on the ice. Now they wanted Chester to make ear protectors to keep their ears warm, too!

With his grandmother's help, Chester began to manufacture ear protectors and continued his business for sixty years. During this time, the ear protectors were improved with adjustable springs and steel hinges to make them fit heads of all sizes. New colors and types of fabrics were used which caused sales to increase rapidly. One season, over 400,000 "Greenwood's Champion Ear Protectors" were made.

Thanks to Chester Greenwood, Farmington, Maine is now known as the "Earmuff Capital of the World." Farmington remembers its inventor each year by having a celebration. Everyone, including many real and stuffed animals, wears earmuffs in honor of Chester Greenwood and his invention.

DIRECTIONS Read each sentence. Draw *one* line under the words which state the *cause*. Draw *two* lines under the words which state the *effect*.

1. Chester didn't want to stop skating because he would miss the fun.

2. His friends would most likely skate all day since their ears didn't seem to get cold very quickly.

3. Because the idea sounded so simple, Chester couldn't believe no one had thought of it earlier.

4. Some of Chester's friends laughed because the ear protectors looked ridiculous.

5. People stopped laughing when they saw how much longer Chester was able to stay outside.

6. Since heads come in all sizes, earmuffs were made with adjustable springs and steel hinges.

REMEMBER A cause makes an effect happen.

A Flash and a Crash

Jagged bolts of lightning flash across the sky! Deafening claps of thunder crash around you! You are witnessing one of nature's most violent moods. In this lesson, you'll read some interesting facts about thunder and lightning. You will also learn about cause and effect, or how some things cause other things to happen.

KEYS to Cause and Effect

When one thing happens, it can cause something else to happen.

LEARN The reason *why* something happens is called the *cause*. *What happens* is called the *effect*. Words like *because, since, when, so,* and *if* are key words that suggest a cause and effect relationship.

DIRECTIONS Read these sentences. Write *cause* on the line if the underlined part tells *why* something happened. Write *effect* if the underlined part tells *what happened*.

1. People do not go swimming during a thunderstorm <u>because they might get struck by lightning.</u>

   _____

2. <u>There were puddles all over the sidewalk this morning</u> because the rain poured for hours last night.

   _____

3. <u>Since it rained so hard</u>, Dad had to pull the car off the road.

   _____

2 Practice With Cause and Effect

DIRECTIONS Read each sentence. Underline the part that tells the *cause*. Remember that the cause tells *why* something happens.

1. We go indoors during a thunderstorm because we might get struck by lightning.

2. Because light travels so fast, we see lightning as soon as it flashes.

3. The crashing sound of thunder is heard because of the lightning.

4. Many pets try to hide during a thunderstorm, since they are afraid of the loud thunder.

5. Since thunder makes a very loud noise, people sometimes forget it is not the dangerous part of a thunderstorm.

DIRECTIONS Read each sentence. Underline the part that tells the *effect*. Remember that the effect tells *what* happens.

1. Buildings can catch on fire because of the extreme heat of lightning.

2. Because they are often taller than anything around them, trees are frequently struck by lightning.

3. You can tell that a thunderstorm is nearby if the thunder is loud and sharp.

4. Because it is so tall, the Empire State Building in New York City is struck by lightning dozens of times each year.

5. When dogs hear thunder, they often shake in fear and seek shelter or the comfort of their owner.

DIRECTIONS Read about thunder and lightning and a man who made something from lightning.

Thunder is caused by lightning. Because it contains so much energy, lightning makes the air around it get very hot. The hot air expands, or swells up, and is pushed in every direction. When the hot air bumps into cooler air, thunder is produced.

Because thunder is only noise, it is not really dangerous. It does, however, tell us how close a storm is. If lightning is nearby, we hear the thunder almost immediately, as loud, sharp claps. If the storm is far away, the thunder makes a long, rumbling sound, and the time between the lightning and the thunder will be much longer.

Benjamin Franklin thought that lightning was electricity and he decided to conduct an experiment to prove it. First, he made a kite. Because he wanted to attract electricity from a bolt of lightning, he attached a piece of wire to the kite. Then he connected a long string to the wire and hung an iron key from the bottom of the string. Franklin expected his kite to attract lightning because it would be higher than the trees and houses around it. He figured that lightning would strike the wire on the kite, and then electricity would travel down the string to the iron key.

Franklin tested his experiment during a thunderstorm. He noticed that a flash of lightning caused the kite string to pull tight. He put his finger near the key and a spark of electricity leaped out, causing him to get a strong electric shock. His experiment was very dangerous, but he proved that lightning was electricity.

DIRECTIONS Read each sentence. Write the words that tell the cause under *Cause* below. Write the words that tell the effect under *Effect* below. The first one is done for you.

1. Franklin thought that lightning was electricity so he conducted an experiment to prove it.

2. Franklin's kite string was pulled tight when a flash of lightning struck it.

3. If lightning is close, the thunder is heard almost immediately.

4. The kite experiment was very dangerous because Franklin could have been killed by the lightning.

5. Because it contains so much energy, lightning makes the air around it get very hot.

6. When hot air bumps into cooler air, there is a noise called thunder.

CAUSE

1. Franklin thought that lightning was electricity

2. _____

3. _____

4. _____

5. _____

6. _____

EFFECT

1. so he conducted an experiment to prove it

2. _____

3. _____

4. _____

5. _____

6. _____

REMEMBER A cause makes an effect happen.

Natural Barriers To Travel

Can't go under it. Can't go through it. Gotta go over it. In this lesson, you'll read about methods of travel and things that get in the way of travel. You'll also learn about how things are alike and different.

 ## 1 KEYS to Comparing and Contrasting

Things can be alike or different or alike *and* different.

LEARN *Comparing* shows how two things or ideas are alike. *Contrasting* shows how things are different.

EXAMPLE Contrast: A small truck has four wheels, but a trailertruck may have as many as eighteen wheels.

Comparison: A city bus and a touring bus can carry many people.

DIRECTIONS Write *1* before each sentence that shows a comparison. Write *2* before a contrast statement.

_____ **1.** Although Amish horse-and-buggies travel with cars on main highways, the horse-driven vehicles are much slower.

_____ **2.** The station wagon and van both have three seats.

_____ **3.** A sports car carries fewer people than a limousine does.

_____ **4.** People travel long distances by train and by car, but car travel allows people to stop and rest when they want.

Practice Comparing and Contrasting

DIRECTIONS Read the list of ten methods of travel. Compare and contrast the methods as you answer the questions below.

airplane   bus

automobile   helicopter

balloon   horse

bicycle   ship

boat   train

1. Which methods of travel have no wheels?

_____

_____

2. Which methods can go over lakes and rivers without touching the water?

_____

_____

_____

3. Which three methods are the slowest?

_____

4. Which kind of transportation carries people only where the wind blows?

_____

5. Which types would you be most likely to use to go from the United States to England?

_____

_____

6. Which methods can go through mountain tunnels?

_____

_____

7. Which means of transportation might you choose to travel to a relative's house thirty miles away?

_____

_____

Read and Apply

Read about how people travel from place to place when nature gets in the way.

Can't go under it. Can't go around it. Gotta go through it! When natural barriers like mountains or water get in the way, people have created solutions such as bridges and tunnels.

The Mont Cenis Tunnel is a route through the Alps Mountains. The tunnel allows trains to go from France to Italy without going all the way around the mountains. Construction of the tunnel, which was completed in 1870, took nearly twenty years. The power drill, a new tool at the time, was used to drill small holes in the mountain. Gunpowder was placed in the holes, and the loose rock was dug out by hand after the blast. Much drilling, blasting, and digging led to easier travel between the two countries.

Rivers, lakes, and canyons are spanned by bridges. The longest bridge span over water is the Lake Pontchartrain Causeway in Louisiana. Built in 1956, the highway goes for 24 miles, or 39 kilometers, across Lake Pontchartrain. A bridge of another kind is the suspension bridge. One of the world's longest suspension bridges spans the San Francisco Bay. The Golden Gate Bridge was opened in 1937 to allow people to travel between the tip of the San Francisco Peninsula to Oakland, a city in a mountain range north of the Bay. Unlike many bridges, a suspension bridge has no supports other than a tower at each end. A giant net was tied below the construction area to protect workers when the 9,000-foot Golden Gate Bridge was being built.

A mountain pass is another way to travel when mountains get in the way. The Khyber Pass is the quickest way to go from Pakistan to Afghanistan. The pass extends for 33 miles, or 53 kilometers, and is the lowest place between two huge mountain ranges. At one point, the pass is only 10 feet, or 3 meters, wide. In addition to a railroad, there is a road for cars and a separate road for camels in the Khyber Pass.

Another famous mountain pass is the Donner Pass which runs through the Sierra Nevada Mountains. This pass gained its name from a group of early pioneers, the Donner Party, who attempted to travel west by wagon train through the mountains to California. The group started through the pass just as heavy snowstorms hit the area. Unable to move onward, they camped there until the storm ended. With little food, they continued to make their way, but only a few of the group succeeded. Because many people died there, the pass was named in their honor.

DIRECTIONS Read each sentence. Write *compare* or *contrast* or *compare/contrast* on the line to tell if two things are being compared or contrasted, or both.

_____ 1. Mountains and water are common barriers to travel.

_____ 2. Some of the Donner Party reached California, but others didn't.

_____ 3. Bridges span both rivers and canyons.

_____ 4. All bridges have supports, but some are supported only at the ends.

_____ 5. Tunnels and passes are ways through mountains.

_____ 6. Although airplanes and ships are both solutions to water barriers, a ship is much slower.

_____ 7. An engine-driven boat is faster than a canoe.

_____ 8. The people of France and Italy were both helped when the Mont Cenis Tunnel was opened.

_____ 9. The Lake Pontchartrain Causeway is longer than the Golden Gate Bridge.

REMEMBER Comparing and contrasting show likenesses and differences.

Furry Scurriers

Lesson **32**

What animal is as small as a crayon and as active as an acrobat? In this lesson, you'll learn about a special way of comparing two things as you read about furry harvest mice who scurry about constantly.

 1 KEYS to Figurative Language

A simile uses *like* or *as* to compare two things.

LEARN Some words do not mean exactly what they say. *Figures of speech* can help you see a picture in your mind. A *simile* is one kind of figure of speech. It compares two things by using the words *like* or *as*.

EXAMPLE The boys looked like pigs. They'd played football on a field as muddy as a barnyard after a heavy rain.

The boys and pigs are alike because both are muddy. The field and a barnyard are alike because both are full of mud.

DIRECTIONS Read each sentence. Write the two things that are being compared and tell how they are alike.

1. Jamie was stubborn as a mule about practicing the piano.

   What two things are being compared? _____ _____

   How are they alike? _____

2. The scouts worked like beavers to gather wood for the campfire.

   What two things are being compared? _____ _____

   How are they alike? _____

Practice With Figurative Language

DIRECTIONS Look for similes as you read each sentence. Underline the words that tell what things are being compared. Then write the letter of the sentence from the box that tells how the things are alike. The first one is done for you.

__b__ **1.** The fur of the harvest mice looks like the <u>ground</u> they live on.

_____ **2.** Harvest mice use their teeth like a nutcracker to nibble through hard and crunchy seeds.

_____ **3.** The tails of harvest mice look like little ropes.

_____ **4.** Harvest mice freeze like statues at the slightest smell or sound of danger.

_____ **5.** Harvest mice are as much fun to watch as a three-ring circus.

_____ **6.** A harvest mouse clings to a grass blade like a toddler clings to its mother.

_____ **7.** Harvest mice seem as wise as owls.

_____ **8.** When a harvest mouse is on a grass blade, the blade swings like a pendulum on a clock.

a. They both hold tightly.
b. They are both brown.
c. They are both smart.
d. They are both entertaining.
e. They both go back and forth.
f. They both break hard things.
g. They are both long and skinny.
h. They are both still.

Read and Apply

Look for the words *like* and *as* for clues to similes as you read the story.

When full-grown, the body of a harvest mouse is only as long as a crayon. Three adult harvest mice would not weigh as much as one slice of cheese! Like a newborn baby, a harvest mouse needs to eat almost constantly. You can find them crunching and munching at any time of the day or night.

A field is a perfect place for harvest mice to build their nests. First, grass is woven to look like a cup. Then the cup is lined with more grass that the mice shred until it is as soft as cotton. The tiny nests of harvest mice hang from grass stalks. The nests are small because a newborn harvest mouse weighs less than a thumbtack.

Watching harvest mice is as much fun as watching a circus. The mice look like midget acrobats performing tricks. They swing and twirl from grass stem to grass stem as swiftly as a trapeze artist changes trapezes. Their long narrow tails swing from side to side.

Harvest mice look like they might fall, but they hold onto the grass by wrapping their tails around the blades. Then they use their hind feet to grab the stems and ride the grass like children on a swing. Their front feet are stretched out and their whiskers are like a spider web in a breeze.

Although harvest mice may look like they're putting on a show, they are actually working. Their scurrying to and fro as if playing hide and seek is really their process of searching for food.

Think about the similes in the story you just read. Circle the letter of the answer that best completes each sentence.

1. The mice look just like acrobats means:
   a. They are in the circus.
   b. They swing easily from blade to blade.
   c. They hold onto ropes.

2. Harvest mice ride the grass like children on a swing means:
   a. Someone pushes them.
   b. They are in a playground.
   c. They move back and forth.

3. Their scurrying looks like they're playing hide and seek means:
   a. They search for each other.
   b. They run to and fro as they search for food.
   c. They are playing a game.

4. They weave the grass to look like a cup means:
   a. The nest is a hollow half-circle.
   b. It would hold a hot drink.
   c. The nest has a handle on it for holding.

5. The mice swing as swiftly as a trapeze artist means:
   a. They easily move in the air from grass blade to grass blade.
   b. They swing on metal bars in the air.
   c. They perform in a tent.

6. Harvest mice eat like newborn babies means:
   a. They drink from a bottle.
   b. They eat around the clock, rather than three meals a day.
   c. They eat very little.

7. Their whiskers are like a spider web in a breeze means:
   a. They are woven in fancy patterns.
   b. They are destroyed by the wind.
   c. They blow in the wind.

8. Harvest mice may look like they're putting on a show means:
   a. They are fun to watch.
   b. They can sing and dance.
   c. They never work.

9. The mice shred the grass until it is as soft as cotton means:
   a. They use cotton to make their nests.
   b. It feels like cement inside their nests.
   c. It feels very soft inside their nests.

REMEMBER A simile is used to compare two things.

Spring Forward, Fall Back

If you live in an area that goes on daylight saving time every spring, you may know the saying, "Spring forward, fall back." In this lesson, you will read about a man who takes credit for inventing that phrase. You will learn other ways to improve your memory.

1 KEYS to Memory Power

Special tricks can help you improve your memory.

LEARN Studying for a test is easier when you know tricks to help you memorize. One trick is to take the first letter of each word of a list you need to remember and use those letters in a way that makes more sense to you.

Do you know that the word *FACE* and the sentence *Every good boy does fine* can help you read music? The first letter of each word of the sentence is the name of a line on the treble clef. Each letter in the word *FACE* is the name of a space between the lines.

The sentence *My very elderly mother just served us nine pizzas* can help you remember the names of the planets. The first letter of each word is also the first letter of the name of a planet: Mercury, Venus, Earth, Mars, Jupiter, Saturn, Uranus, Neptune, Pluto.

DIRECTIONS Do you know a man named ROY G. BIV? Another name for ROY could be Mr. Rainbow, since each letter of ROY's name is the same as the first letter of a color of the rainbow: Red, Orange, Yellow, Green, Blue, Indigo, Violet.

Cover the top of the page. Use ROY G. BIV to help you write the colors of the rainbow from memory.

_____   _____   _____

_____   _____   _____

2 Practice With Memory

DIRECTIONS What kind of memory system works best for you? You might need to memorize a list of exports of a particular country for social studies. For science, it may be a list of the parts of a system of the body or the plants in a particular class. Try two different ways to memorize a list of unrelated items. Decide which system works best for you.

SYSTEM 1: Read it over.

Maybe you're a person who learns best by reading something over several times. Read List 1 three times. Then cover it up and write as many items as you can remember on the lines.

SYSTEM 2: Write it down.

Some people remember best when they write things down. On a piece of scrap paper, write List 2 three times. Then hide the paper and cover the list. Write as many items as you can remember on the lines.

List 1: pencil, sofa, bear, television, doll, car, bottle, bathtub, newspaper, fork

List 2: roller coaster, table, train, monkey, football, star, glasses, stairs, lake, apple

_____   _____

_____   _____

_____   _____

_____   _____

Most people enjoy being on daylight saving time in the summer. It gives them an extra hour of daylight in the evening to have fun or work around the house. What most people don't like are the two weekends, one in the spring and one in the fall, when clocks need to be changed. It's always hard to remember whether to turn the hands forward one hour or back one hour.

In the 1960s, one man thought of a way to make it easier to make the change. The man was a high school psychology teacher in Cleveland, Ohio. He was teaching a lesson about mnemonic devices. That's a long way to say memory tricks. The teacher wanted to think of his own memory trick, and that's when he thought of the phrase "Spring forward, fall back" to remind us to turn the clock forward in the spring and back again in the fall. Today that phrase is used all over the country.

How did so many people find out about it?

"Word of mouth," says the teacher. His students told a few people. Those people told a few more. Pretty soon everyone was using his memory trick to stay on time during daylight saving time.

DIRECTIONS Try a trick of your own to improve your memory. Remember the lists you had to memorize on page 138? This trick will make memorizing lists easier. It may take some practice, but it will be worth it.

Make a mind picture that links each pair of words in the list. The stranger the picture, the longer you will remember it. Read the list of words. Then turn the page to see how the trick, or mnemonic device, works.

List 3: dog, picture, candle, shoe, pillow, teacher, tree, baseball, duck, baby

DIRECTIONS Read the descriptions of some mind pictures for List 3. Close your eyes and try to see each picture in your mind.

dog-picture: a dog wearing a smock and painting at an easel

picture-candle: a candle flame beginning to burn the edge of a picture

candle-shoe: the same candle using an old shoe as a candle holder

shoe-pillow: you—wearing pillows on your feet instead of shoes

pillow-teacher: your teacher teaching a class of pillows instead of students

teacher-tree: a tree writing on a chalkboard

tree-baseball: a baseball player swinging a tree instead of a bat

baseball-duck: a duck hatching a baseball instead of an egg

duck-baby: a nest with three baby ducks and one human baby

Now cover the mind pictures. Write as many items as you can remember on the lines.

_____

_____

_____

_____

DIRECTIONS Make up your own mind pictures for the list below. Make the pictures as silly as you can. Test your memory by covering the list and writing as many items as you can on the lines.

List 4: cup, T-shirt, sled, elephant, king, refrigerator, blanket, book, flowerpot, lamp

_____

_____

_____

_____

REMEMBER Tricks can help you memorize.

Don't Get Lost!

Everyone knows being lost is no fun! That's why we have maps. Maps keep us from getting lost. In this lesson, you'll learn to use a map. Then you'll help others find their way, too.

1 KEYS to Maps

Maps show information about places.

LEARN A map's *legend* tells what each *symbol* on the map means. Most maps have a compass near the legend. The *compass* tells you which directions on the map are north, south, east and west. If north is up, or at the top of a map, write the direction that is

1. down or at the bottom. _____   **2.** to the right. _____

DIRECTIONS Use the legend and map to answer the questions.

1. Which direction would you go from Wharton to Crystal City? _____

2. What town has a hospital? _____

3. Which town is closest to a campground? _____

4. Could you get from Mathis to Albion by railroad? _____

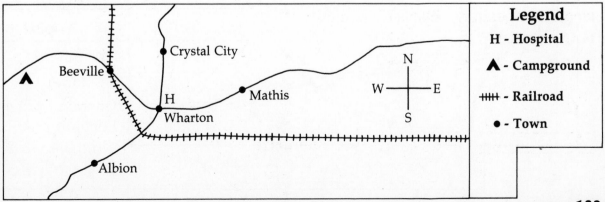

Maps **133**

2 Practice With Maps

DIRECTIONS Cartographers are people who make maps. Cartographers use letters and numbers on maps to make it easier to locate places. Each city on the map is listed alphabetically in an index by a letter and number. If you read "Burrows C3" in the map index, you will find Burrows on the map by pointing to the letter C on the side of the map, then running your finger across the map until it is under the number 3. Burrows will be found near that spot.

Use the map, its legend and index to complete the work below.

1. Using the index, locate the dot for each town. Write its name on the map.

2. Interstate 84 and State Highway 57 meet in this town.

_____

3. Which direction do you travel from Burrows to Clymers?

_____

4. How should Sica be listed in the map index?

_____

5. Which highway takes you from Edgeton to Clymers?

_____

6. How should Sterling be listed in the map index?

_____

7. What town is between Sica and Reilly on State Highway 57?

_____

8. Which town has an airport and a hospital?

_____

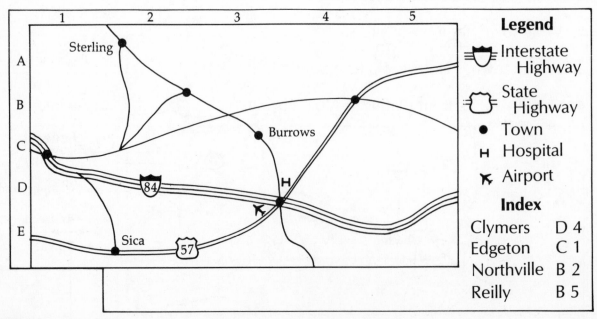

Read and Apply

DIRECTIONS Study the map. Then read each sentence below and circle *T* for true or *F* for false.

1. Newsville and Black River Falls are near campgrounds.　　T　　F
2. Your flight from Eau Claire could land in Blaire.　　T　　F
3. A map index for this map would show Eleva located at E4.　　T　　F
4. Black River Falls probably has a train station.　　T　　F
5. You'd travel Interstate Highway 94 from Galesville to Blair.　　T　　F
6. Two county parks are near Eau Claire.　　T　　F
7. Fountain City is located near D1 on this map.　　T　　F
8. Granton is a large city.　　T　　F

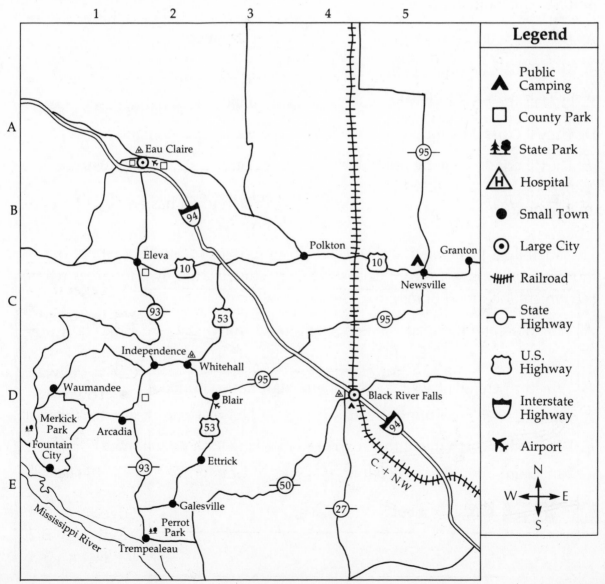

Use the map on the previous page to answer the questions.

1. Jamie is in the Black River Falls hospital with a broken leg. His grandmother wants to drive over to visit him. Grandmother lives in Arcadia and needs directions to the hospital.

   A. She should take State Highway _____ .

   B. She will be traveling north and _____ .

   C. She will go through the town of _____ .

   D. She will turn _____ and go southeast on Interstate _____ .

2. A family of campers is lost. They have stopped in Galesville to ask how to get to their camp site in Newsville.

   A. The shortest way is to go _____ on U.S. Highway _____ .

   B. They'll pass a county park site at _____ .

   C. In Blair they will turn onto _____ Highway _____ .

   D. They'll cross a major highway called _____ .

   E. They'll continue going north and _____ on _____ Highway _____ .

   F. They'll cross a _____ before reaching Newsville.

3. Tina's family is planning to move to be closer to Perrot State Park where her mother works as a forestry specialist. They're studying the map for areas where they might look for a home.

   A. Which area of the map will they want to be studying?

   B 2   B 5   E 2   C 4

   B. Which town might be a good place to start house hunting?

   Eleva   Trempealeau   Newsville   Whitehall

   C. What other town might they explore in looking for a new home?

   Eau Claire   Polkton   Granton   Galesville

A map is a guide to a place.

All In Good Health

What is necessary for good health? In this lesson, you'll read about some good health habits as you learn about graphs.

▲1 KEYS to Graphs

Facts are compared on a graph.

LEARN Facts on a graph can be compared at a glance. Pictures or symbols are used on a *picture graph*. Part of a picture or symbol means part of a larger number. The *key* tells what the picture or symbol means.

EXAMPLE

Seafood Eaten in January

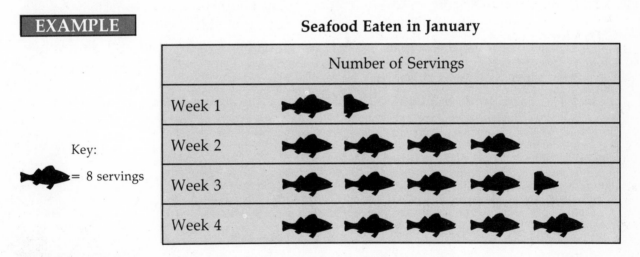

Key:

= 8 servings

DIRECTIONS Use the facts in the graph to complete the sentences.

1. One-half fish means _____ servings of seafood.

2. A total of _____ servings of seafood were eaten the first week.

3. During week _____, the most servings of seafood were eaten.

4. Annie's class ate _____ more servings of seafood during the last week than the first week.

2 Practice With Graphs

DIRECTIONS A *circle graph,* or *pie graph,* is used to compare one part to a whole group. Each labeled part of the pie tells about one part of the whole. Read about Jerry's record of his exercise during the month of April. Study the graph. Mark an X before each statement that is true.

When Jerry's class studied diet and exercise in health class, Ms. Koontz asked the students to keep a record of their exercise for a month. At the end of the month, Jerry made a graph to show how his total of 84 active hours was spent.

_____ **1.** Jerry spent the most time riding his bicycle.

_____ **2.** He played soccer and softball the same amount of time.

_____ **3.** He swam more than he played soccer.

_____ **4.** He did more walking than swimming.

_____ **5.** Yard work was done for fewer hours than any other activity.

_____ **6.** Jerry exercised by swimming more than anything else.

_____ **7.** Jerry spent 18 hours walking.

_____ **8.** Jerry bicycled 5 hours less than he played soccer.

_____ **9.** He exercised a total of 84 hours during the month.

How I Exercise

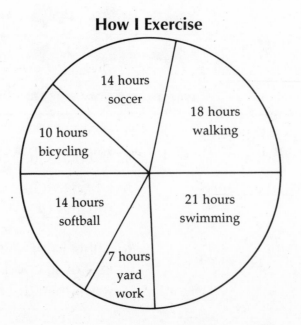

14 hours soccer

18 hours walking

10 hours bicycling

14 hours softball

7 hours yard work

21 hours swimming

3 Read and Apply

DIRECTIONS Facts can be shown on a *bar graph*. Read the bar graph by following the bar across the graph to its end. Read the paragraph and study the graph. Then answer the questions below.

As Kristy's class learned about the foods their bodies need for good health, they also read about foods that people often call junk foods. Some of Kristy's classmates weren't sure how often they ate junk food. They decided to keep a record of how many times they ate junk food during a two-week period.

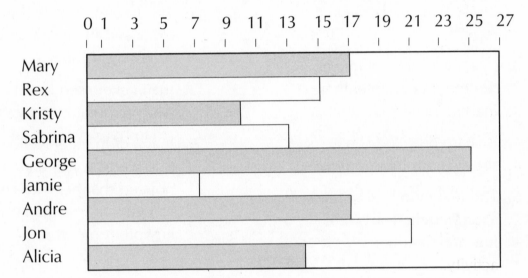

How Many Times We Ate Junk Food

1. Who ate junk food the least?

   _____

2. Which two students ate these foods the same number of times in the two-week period?

   _____

3. How many times did Sabrina eat junk foods?

   _____

4. Who probably ate no candy and drank no pop for at least seven of the fourteen days?

   _____

5. Who ate junk food the most times?

   _____

6. What is the difference between Rex's and Jon's totals?

   _____

Line graphs show how facts change over a period of time. As on a bar graph, labels at the side and bottom give you information. Facts are shown on a line graph as dots on grid lines. When the dots are connected in order, it is easy to see changes. Read the paragraph and study the line graph. Then write *T* for true or *F* for false before each statement below.

Juana wanted to see if her amount of exercise changed from month to month. To find out, she kept a record of the number of hours she played a sport or did another type of exercise. She recorded the total hours of exercise each month.

_____ **1.** Juana was the most active in the month of June.

_____ **2.** Juana never exercised more than 105 hours in a month.

_____ **3.** Juana was more active in the month of September than in May.

_____ **4.** A sharp drop in exercise is shown from June to July.

_____ **5.** The two months that Juana exercised the least were July and October.

_____ **6.** Juana exercised fifteen hours more in June than in May.

_____ **7.** The two months that Juana exercised the most were August and June.

_____ **8.** Juana exercised less than seventy hours one month.

_____ **9.** Juana didn't feel well for one week in July and noticed that her total that month was less than during any other month.

My Exercise

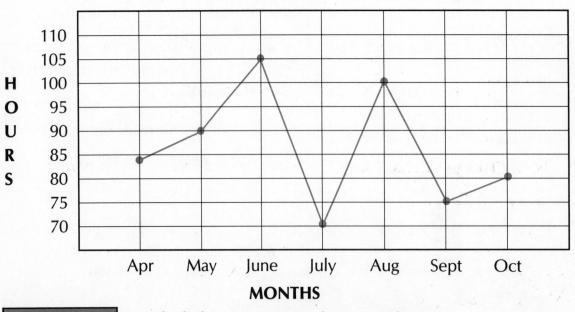

MONTHS

REMEMBER Graphs help you compare facts at a glance.

A Matter of Time

Why do you have to change the time on your watch as you travel across the country on a long trip? In this lesson, you'll read about time zone differences as you learn to read facts on a table.

1 KEYS to Tables

Facts are often organized in a table.

LEARN | A table of facts may list *numbers, symbols,* or *words*. A *title* tells the topic, and *headings* begin a row or column. To find a fact, go *across a row* and *down a column*.

Time in Different Time Zones			
Pacific	Mountain	Central	Eastern
1:00	2:00	3:00	4:00
3:00	4:00	5:00	6:00
5:00	6:00	7:00	8:00

DIRECTIONS Use the table to complete the statements.

1. When it is 6:00 in the Eastern zone, it is __4:00__ in Mountain time.

2. At 3:00 in Chicago's Central time, a clock in San Francisco's Pacific zone would say __1:00__.

3. Eastern time is __3__ hours ahead of, or later than, Pacific time.

4. Four o'clock in the Mountain time zone is __5:00__ in Central time, __3:00__ in Pacific time, and __6:00__ in Eastern time.

2 Practice With Tables

DIRECTIONS The table shows the time zone of each of the ten largest cities in the United States. The cities are listed from the largest, New York City, to the smallest, San Antonio. Use the table to answer each question below.

Time Zones of 10 Largest Cities in U.S.				
City	Pacific	Mountain	Central	Eastern
New York, New York				X
Los Angeles, California	X			
Chicago, Illinois			X	
Houston, Texas			X	
Philadelphia, Pennsylvania				X
Detroit, Michigan				X
Dallas, Texas			X	
San Diego, California	X			
Phoenix, Arizona		X		
San Antonio, Texas			X	

1. Which time zone includes most of the nation's ten largest cities?

   Central ✓

2. The California cities are in what time zone?

   Pacific ✓

3. Are Detroit and Phoenix in the same time zone?

   NO ✓

4. Which zone includes the smallest number of the nation's ten largest cities?

   Mountain ✓

5. What zone includes the cities in Texas?

   Central ✓

6. The nation's ninth largest city is in which zone?

   mountian ✓

7. Which cities are in the Pacific and Mountain time zones?

   Los Angeles, California ✓
   San Diego California, Phoenix Arizona

8. Which zone includes the second and eighth largest U.S. cities?

   Pacific ✓

DIRECTIONS Read about how time zones came to be.

Until about one hundred years ago, the sun was the only true clock. People looked at the position of the sun to tell the time. When the sun was at its peak overhead, they guessed it was noon and set their clocks for twelve o'clock. Needless to say, few clocks showed the same time. This seemed fine to most people who only needed to know *about* what time it was.

Telling time by the sun caused problems for other people, though. The railroads made their schedules by their clocks, but passengers' clocks were all different. This meant that people might miss trains because their watches were a few minutes slow.

A college professor in St. Louis saw the need for uniform time. He suggested that a large, red, metal ball be dropped down a pole in each town at noon every day. This would allow people to set their clocks and watches at the same time. Many cities used his idea, but because the sun was seen in its peak position at different times in different towns, noon was not at the same time everywhere. Problems remained.

Charles Dowd, another teacher, suggested that the United States be divided into four time zones. William F. Allen, a railroad engineer, agreed with Dowd. Each zone, they said, should stretch across the United States the distance the sun travels in one hour. Railroad officials liked the idea, and they agreed to reset all clocks in the country on November 18, 1883. The time zones were named the eastern, central, mountain, and pacific zones.

Although people used the official time zones, it was another thirty-five years before time zones became law. The Standard Time Act was passed by Congress on March 19, 1918.

The original time zone boundary lines were fairly straight. A boundary could go through the middle of a town, between two neighbor's houses, or even between a kitchen and living room in a single house! People wanted to be on the same time as everyone around them. This problem was mostly solved by changing the straighter lines to zigzag lines. In some places today, however, people of neighboring towns find their watches are different by one hour.

DIRECTIONS Use the table as you circle *T* for true or *F* for false for each statement below.

Hour Changes in Time From City to City				
	Los Angeles	Montreal	St. Louis	Pittsburgh
Denver	Subtract 1	Add 2	Add 1	Add 2
Miami	Subtract 3	Same	Subtract 1	Same
Seattle	Same	Add 3	Add 2	Add 3
Washington, D.C.	Subtract 3	Same	Subtract 1	Same
Boston	Subtract 3	Same	Subtract 1	Same
Cheyenne	Subtract 1	Add 2	Add 1	Add 2

1. You need to set your watch ahead three hours when traveling from Seattle to Montreal. T F

2. There is a two hour difference between the times in Cheyenne and St. Louis. T F

3. When going from Seattle to Los Angeles, you do not cross any time zone boundaries. T F

4. Denver and St. Louis have a one-hour time difference. T F

5. When it is 12:00 midnight in Montreal, it is also midnight in Denver. T F

REMEMBER Tables organize facts.

Detective Work

Scientists and law-enforcement offi-cers work to solve mysteries. In this lesson, you'll read about how these professionals often work together as crimebusters. You'll learn to solve mysteries of your own as you practice using the dictionary to do some wordbusting.

△1 KEYS to Using the Dictionary

A dictionary gives information about words.

LEARN A *dictionary* is a wordbuster's best tool. It tells the meaning of a word, how to pronounce it, and how the word can be used. If the word can be used as a noun, the abbreviation *n.* is given. The abbreviation *v.* means the word can be used as a verb, and *adj.* means it can be used as an adjective. The most common use of the word is given first.

DIRECTIONS Read the dictionary entry. Circle the answer to each question.

> **de·tec·tive** (di tek′tiv) **n.** a person, usually on a police force, whose work is trying to solve crimes, getting secret information, etc. ◆**adj.** of detectives and their work.

1. How is the word used most commonly?
   a. noun   **b.** verb   **c.** adjective

2. How many syllables are in the word?
   a. four   **b.** three   **c.** five

3. Which syllable is accented when the word is pronounced?
   a. first   **b.** third   **c.** second

Practice With Dictionaries

DIRECTIONS Dictionary entries also tell how a longer word is divided into syllables. This information is helpful when you're writing a word that will not fit at the end of a line.

pro·fes·sion·al   de·tec·tive

Use the dictionary entries to help you do some wordbusting. Answer the questions.

lab·o·ra·to·ry (lab′rə tôr′ē *or* lab′ər ə tôr′ē) **n.** a room or building where scientific work or tests are carried on, or where chemicals, drugs, etc. are prepared. —*pl.* **lab′o·ra·to′ries**

chem·i·cal (kem′i k′l) **adj.** 1 of or in chemistry [a *chemical* process]. 2 made by or used in chemistry [*chemical* compounds]. ◆**n.** any substance used in chemistry or got by a chemical process [Various *chemicals* are used in making plastics.] —**chem′i·cal·ly adv.**

crim·i·nal (krim′ə n′l) **adj.** 1 being a crime; that is a crime [a *criminal* act]. 2 having to do with crime [*criminal* law]. ◆**n.** a person guilty of a crime. —**crim′·i·nal·ly adv.**

stand·ard (stan′dərd) **n.** 1 something set up as a rule or model with which other things like it are to be compared 2 a flag, banner, etc., as of a military group or a nation 3 an upright support ◆**adj.** 1 that is a standard, rule, or model 2 not special or extra; ordinary 3 accepted as good or proper.

1. Write each of the words to show how it is divided into syllables.

_____

_____

_____

_____

2. The word *chemical* can be used as

a _____

or _____ .

3. Which use of the word *standard* is most common?

_____

4. Which word's first two letters have the *k* sound?

_____

5. Which word is most commonly used as a noun, although it can be an adjective?

_____

6. Which word can only be used as a noun?

_____

7. Write the meaning of the word *criminal* when used as a noun.

_____

_____

8. Which word has two accent marks?

_____

DIRECTIONS Read how some crimebusters solved a mystery.

Forensic medicine is combining medicine with law. New discoveries in forensic medicine have helped crime fighters do their jobs. Finger-printing, which was first used in 1911, is now a standard part of any investigation. Law enforcement officers and scientists also use computers, laser beams, and various chemical tests in their work.

Scientists recently had the gruesome task of trying to identify some remains as the body of Joseph Mengele, the world's most wanted Nazi war criminal. The sparse evidence consisted of seven teeth, some clumps of hair, a pile of bones, and a decaying pair of trousers.

It was reported that Mengele died in 1979 in Brazil at the age of 78. Laboratory tests showed that the skeleton matched Mengele's. Examination of the skull showed a space between the two upper front teeth. Survivors of the camp where Mengele had tortured countless people during World War II, recalled a gap between the Nazi doctor's teeth. The pieces of the puzzle were falling into place.

Dental records proved helpful in the investigation. Each person's teeth have different root shapes and show differences in the way they wear down from use. The dental records of Mengele's teeth were compared with the evidence, and they were a perfect match. A study of the bones also showed that the remains were those of a man who was the same height as Mengele.

When the forensic experts combined all their evidence, the identification was complete. The 40-year search for the notorious war criminal was over.

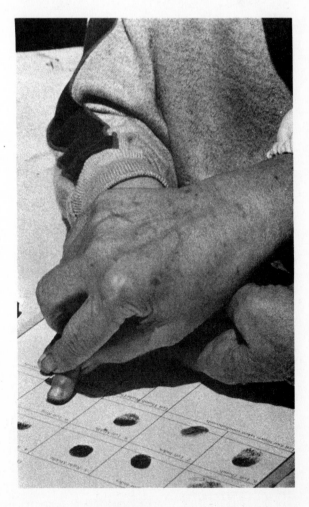

DIRECTIONS Read the dictionary entries. Then use the entries as you answer the questions below.

de·cay (di kā′) **v.** **1** to become rotten by the action of bacteria. **2** to fall into ruins; become no longer sound, powerful, rich, beautiful, etc. **3** to break down so that there are fewer radioactive atoms. ♦**n.** **1** a rotting or falling into ruin. **2** the breaking down of radioactive material so that there are fewer radioactive atoms.

en·hance (in hans′) **v.** to make better, greater, etc. **en·hanced′, en·hanc′ing**

fo·ren·sic (fə ren′sik) **adj.** of or used in a law court or debate.

grue·some (groo′səm) **adj.** causing fear and disgust; horrible.

re·call (ri kôl′) **v.** **1** to bring back to mind; remember. **2** to call back; order to return. **3** to take back; withdraw or cancel. **n.** (*also* rē′kôl) **1** the act of recalling. **2** the right of citizens to vote an official out of office, using petitions to call for such a vote.

sparse (spärs) **adj.** thinly spread or scattered; not thick or crowded. **sparse′ly adv. —spar′si·ty n.**

1. Which word means *to remember?*

_____

2. Which word's verb form means *to rot?*

_____

3. What verb means *to make better?*

_____

4. What word's final c has the sound of k?

_____

5. What three words are most commonly used as verbs?

_____

_____

6. Which word has three syllables?

_____

7. Which four words have two syllables each?

_____

_____

_____

_____

8. Which three words are used only as adjectives?

_____

_____

_____

9. Which two-syllable word is pronounced with the accent on its first syllable?

_____

REMEMBER A dictionary is a guidebook to words.

148 Dictionary

Books of Knowledge

Although all books contain information, a special kind of reference book contains so much information it can't be held in one book. In this lesson, you'll learn about sets of books that are full of facts and information.

1 KEYS to Encyclopedias

Encyclopedias contain facts about all kinds of subjects.

LEARN In a *general encyclopedia,* all kinds of subjects are arranged in alphabetical order in *volumes,* or separate books. A separate volume, the *index,* lists each subject. A section called *Related Articles* is found at the end of some articles to help you find additional information.

DIRECTIONS Read the list of words. Then read each sentence and write the letter of the correct word on the line.

a. Index   **c.** Related Articles   **e.** Volume
b. Alphabetically   **d.** General Encyclopedia

_____ **1.** This will help you find other articles about a topic.

_____ **2.** This is any one book of a set.

_____ **3.** One volume tells me where to find each subject.

_____ **4.** Subjects are listed this way in an encyclopedia.

_____ **5.** This includes articles on all kinds of subjects.

DIRECTIONS Information about a subject can usually be found under more than one topic in an encyclopedia. Information on race cars, for example, might be found under *cars, races, racing, sports,* and other related words. Read each sentence and underline every key word or phrase that you might use to find more information.

1. Evergreen trees keep their leaves all year long.

2. Shoulder pads and a helmet protect athletes in some sports.

3. Michelangelo's Statue of David stands in Florence, Italy.

4. Some of Walt Disney's cartoon characters are more than fifty years old.

5. Graphics are fun to create on a computer keyboard and monitor.

6. The bulbs of perennial flowers, like the tulip, sprout new growth each year.

7. Good nutrition and plenty of exercise are keys to fitness.

8. Paintings, drawings, sculptures, and other works of art are on exhibit in art museums.

9. The Pittsburgh Pirates play baseball at Three Rivers Stadium.

Read and Apply

Read more about encyclopedias and their contents.

Some subjects are very narrow and can be explained in a few paragraphs in an encyclopedia. For other subjects, however, there is an abundance of information. An article on art could be very lengthy because there are many types of art.

In order to explain what art is, an art specialist would write about different artists whose talents and styles have contributed to the field of art. A reader who is looking for information about art may want to learn about the history of art, why art is important in our world, how art is enjoyed by people, where art can be viewed, or a host of other information about the subject.

Since people do not read encyclopedias from "cover to cover," it is helpful to have *subheadings* in articles. Subheadings in an article on art might be titled *history, kinds of art, art museums,* or *artists.* Subheadings help us scan, or move the eyes quickly, over an article to find a subheading for particular information we want to read.

Specialized encyclopedias are written about some subjects because there is so much information available. These specialized sets may have as little as one volume or as many volumes as needed to include all the information. *Science and Technology, Lands and Peoples, U.S. Presidents, Mammals,* and *About the Author* are some titles of specialized encyclopedias.

1. An encyclopedia
   a. gives many facts about each topic.
   b. may be in one or many volumes.
   c. contains short and lengthy articles.
   d. all of the above.

2. Subheadings in an encyclopedia article
   a. help you find specific facts about a subject.
   b. guide you to additional information in other volumes.
   c. help you read an encyclopedia from "cover to cover."
   d. ask questions to help you get the most from your reading.

3. Specialized encyclopedias are written because
   a. there is not enough information about a subject.
   b. there is an abundance of information about a subject.
   c. people read every word on every page.
   d. none of the above.

4. There are many short articles in an encyclopedia because
   a. no one knows how to explain the subject.
   b. people would not read a longer article.
   c. some subjects can be explained in a few paragraphs.
   d. there are no specialists to write about the subject.

5. Information in an encyclopedia.
   a. may be found under several different headings.
   b. may be located by using an index.
   c. may be grouped under subheadings.
   d. all of the above.

REMEMBER Information may be under several topics in an encyclopedia.

Book Search

Hunting for a good book is fun, but only if you understand the clues that will lead you to it. In this lesson, you'll learn three clues for finding any book in the library.

 ## KEYS to the Card Catalog

The card catalog has three cards for each book.

LEARN The *card catalog* contains a *subject* card, a *title* card, and an *author* card for each book in the library. If you know the author, the title, or the subject of the book, you can find its card. Each card gives you information about the book and tells where the book is shelved in the library.

DIRECTIONS Read the author card below. The *call number* is $\frac{535}{F}$ for a science book. Write the other information on the lines.

AUTHOR CARD
535 Freeman, Mary and Ira
F   Fun Experiments with Lights
Random House (1963)
60 pp. illus.

1. Title _____

_____

2. Author _____

_____

3. Publisher _____

_____

4. Publication date _____

5. Number of pages _____

DIRECTIONS Two other cards can be found in the card catalog for the book *Fun Experiments with Lights,* by Mary and Ira Freeman. While the author card was located in the *F* drawer, the subject card would be found in the *L* drawer for the subject, *light*. The title card would be found in the *F* drawer, since the first main word of the book's title begins with *F*. Use the information from the author card on the previous page along with these subject and title cards to answer the questions below.

SUBJECT CARD
535   Light experiments
F   Freeman, Mary and Ira
Fun Experiments with Lights
Random House (1963)
60 pp. illus.

TITLE CARD
535   Fun Experiments with Lights
F   Freeman, Mary and Ira
Random House (1963)
60 pp. illus.

1. Which of the three cards lists the book's title first?

_____

2. Which card lists the author's name first?

_____

3. What does the $\frac{535}{F}$ mean?

_____

_____

4. Which of the three cards would be found in the *F* drawer of the card catalog?

_____

_____

5. Why are the authors' names *not* listed first on some of the cards?

_____

_____

6. What letter would be on the drawer of the card catalog for each of the cards?

Subject _____

Author _____

Title _____

7. Could you find this book if you only knew the publisher?

_____

Read and Apply

DIRECTIONS Read each brief description of a book or other material you might search for in the library. Circle the name of the card you would need to find. Then write the letter of the card catalog drawer where you'd find that card.

_____ **1.** A book by Johanna Hurwitz.

    Subject

    Title

    Author

_____ **2.** A book about wood.

    Subject

    Title

    Author

_____ **3.** A book of poetry.

    Subject

    Title

    Author

_____ **4.** A book written by Mary Q. Steele and published in 1979.

    Subject

    Title

    Author

_____ **5.** Any information on mytho-logical characters.

    Subject

    Title

    Author

_____ **6.** Any of Lois Lowry's books.

    Subject

    Title

    Author

_____ **7.** _The Reluctant Dragon,_ whose illustrator is Ernest H. Shepard.

    Subject

    Title

    Author

_____ **8.** A 96-page book called _Soup._

    Subject

    Title

    Author

Use the following cards from a card catalog to tell if each of the following statements is true or false. Circle *T* for true or *F* for false.

1
Fic   ANIMALS-Stories
W   White, E. B.
Charlotte's web
illustrated by Garth Williams
Harper & Row (1952)

2
589   Forest and Woodland
C   Collins, Stephen
Creative Educational
Society (1967)
125 pp. illus.

3
809.7   Doane, Pelagie
D   Poems of praise
J. B. Lippincott (1955)
136 pp. illus.

1. Card 3 is an author card.   T   F

2. Stephen Collins is the author of *Forest and Woodland*.   T   F

3. Card 2 would be found in the *C* drawer of the card catalog.   T   F

4. Card 1 is a subject card.   T   F

5. Another card for E. B. White's book would be found in the *C* drawer of the card catalog.   T   F

6. Other cards for the poetry book would be found in the *L* drawer and the *J* drawer.   T   F

7. Only one of these books has pictures.   T   F

8. The card about a book published by Harper & Row is a title card.   T   F

9. Two of these books are non-fiction books.   T   F

10. You would find a subject card for Collins' book in the *F* drawer of the card catalog.   T   F

REMEMBER Look for a subject, title, or author card in the card catalog.

Imagination and Reality

All books can be separated into two groups, one about things of the imagination and the other about things in reality. In this lesson, you'll learn how books of real and imaginary information are organized in the library.

1 KEYS to Fiction and Non-fiction

Fiction is imaginary, while non-fiction is real.

LEARN *Fiction* books contain stories that never really happened. The stories, even though some may seem real, were made up by authors. *Non-fiction* books are about real people, places, or things. They are filled with facts the author has gathered and believes to be true.

DIRECTIONS Read each sentence. Write *F* on the line if the information is from a fiction book. Write *NF* if the sentence is from a non-fiction book.

_____ **1.** Sharks come in many shapes and sizes.

_____ **2.** The kings and queens in the deck of cards danced merrily.

_____ **3.** Meow, the cat, has the most lines in the play.

_____ **4.** Aquaman used his power to save the ship from certain disaster.

_____ **5.** Computers are widely used for work and for play.

_____ **6.** The cheetah is the fastest land animal in the world.

_____ **7.** The small girl cleverly overcame the giant Cyclops.

Practice With Fiction and Non-fiction

DIRECTIONS A fiction book has *Fic* for *fiction* on its spine above the first letter of the author's last name. Librarians arrange fiction books alphabetically in the fiction section. Write the correct information on the lines of each book's spine. On the line above each book title, number the book to show its correct order on the library shelves. The first one is done for you.

9
A Taste of
Blackberries

Doris Smith

Fic

S

Freckle
Juice

Judy Blume

Soup

Robert Peck

Fire Storm

Robb White

Peter Potts

Clifford
Hicks

Luke Was
There

Eleanor
Clymer

Mr. Popper's
Penguins

Richard and
Florence
Atwater

My Father's
Dragon

Ruth Gannett

The Blue Cat
of Castle Town

Catherine
Coblentz

Summer of
the Monkeys

Wilson Rawls

Read and Apply

DIRECTIONS Read how non-fiction books are organized in a library.

Most libraries use the *Dewey Decimal System* to organize non-fiction books. Melvil Dewey was a librarian who saw a need for a way to organize every non-fiction book in the library. In 1876, Mr. Dewey started a numbering system that is still used today.

There are ten subject areas in the Dewey Decimal System. Each group has its own set of numbers. A book's *call number* tells what subject the book is about. For example, a book about planting flowers would have a call number that is between 600 and 699. Books about sports would have call numbers in the 700s. A book with a call number of 075 would be a reference book. Books are shelved in the library in numerical order. This makes it easy to find any non-fiction book.

Numbers	Subject	Kinds of Books
000–099	General	Encyclopedias, computer books
100–199	Philosophy	Dreams, self-help
200–299	Religion	Mythology, religion
300–399	Social Sciences	Costumes, money, manners, fairy tales
400–499	Language	Dictionaries, words, languages
500–599	Sciences	Animals, mathematics, plants, science
600–699	Technology	Human body, gardening, cooking, airplanes
700–799	Arts	Photography, sports, games, crafts, music, art
800–899	Literature	Poetry, plays, jokes
900–999	Geography and History	Atlases, history, geography, travel

Use the Dewey Decimal System you just read about to write the subject and number group for each book title below. The first one is done for you.

Non-fiction Titles	Subject	Number Group
1. World Famous Ballets	Arts	700–799
2. A Trip to the Virgin Islands		
3. Using Solar Power for Heat		
4. Bubbles, A Book of Poems		
5. Childcraft Encyclopedia		
6. Greek and Roman Myths		
7. Planets of the Universe		
8. Toto, Boy of Kenya		
9. The Joy of Cooking		
10. First Book of Sign Language		
11. Computer Wisdom		
12. Teach Yourself to Learn		

DIRECTIONS Non-fiction books about the same topic are shelved together. The books are placed in alphabetical order by the first letter of the author's last name. Number the science books in order as they should be shelved.

	Title	Author	Dewey Number
_____	1. Birds of Africa	Cecil Bates	598
_____	2. First Book of Song Birds	Ardess Seena	598
_____	3. Ostrich Farms	Timothy Wells	598
_____	4. Birds in Flight	Mary Mueller	598
_____	5. Parrots of the Busch	LoRayne Schmidt	598

REMEMBER All books are either fiction or non-fiction.

Simplicity

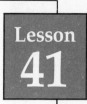

"Keep it simple." You've probably heard this often. Maybe "keep it simple" is what you would like to say when you are learning a new skill.

In this lesson, you will learn to keep it simple as you use a method of note-taking called mapping. You will learn about some people who choose to live a life of simplicity.

 1 KEYS to Mapping

An outline map helps you picture important ideas.

LEARN Notes are short statements which restate important ideas in a simple way. Mapping is an easy way to take notes and remember those important ideas. The lines help you see how ideas are related.

Mapping helps you as you read. It also helps you after you finish reading. As you read, mapping helps you concentrate and understand what you have read. After you finish reading, your map helps you remember the important information. You will use your map when it's time to review what you have read.

DIRECTIONS Study the outline map. Reread the paragraph you just read. Underline the phrases used in the map.

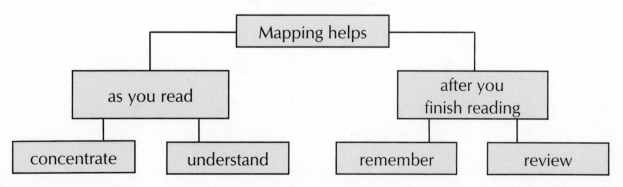

② Practice Mapping

   An outline map makes your notes look like a mobile. The main idea is in the center at the top of the map. Under the main idea are boxes containing the subtopics. Details that tell more about each subtopic belong in the boxes below the subtopics. The lines show how the subtopics and details relate to each other and to the main idea.

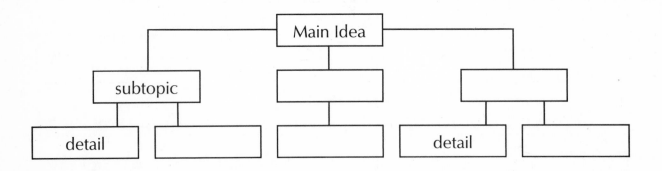

DIRECTIONS Now read the paragraph below and complete the map by filling in the real subtopics and details. Some boxes have been filled in for you.

   These tips will help you take good notes. You need to be neat so you can read what you wrote later. Your notes should be brief so you can review them quickly. Write notes in your own words so they make sense to you. When you have taken good notes, you can use them to save time when you need to review.

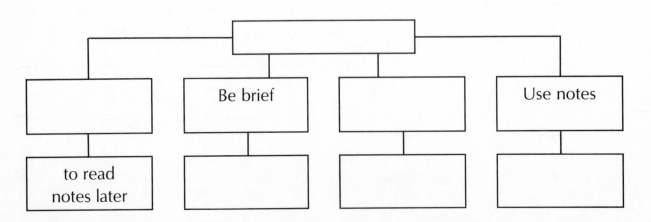

3 Read and Apply

DIRECTIONS Read the paragraphs about a group of people who chose a life of simplicity. Use the underlined information to complete the outline maps.

In the early 1700's, a group of Amish people fled from their homeland, Switzerland. They resettled in North America. Today most Amish communities are found around Ontario, Canada, and in the midwestern United States.

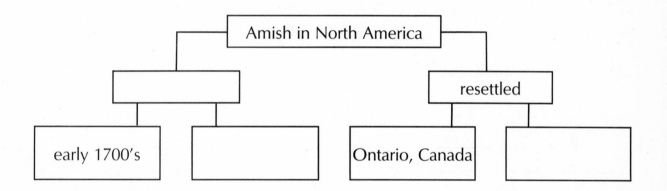

The Amish were searching for religious freedom in the new land. They also searched for good farmland. Farming, they felt, would allow them to live the life of simplicity they value. It would also encourage close-knit family life.

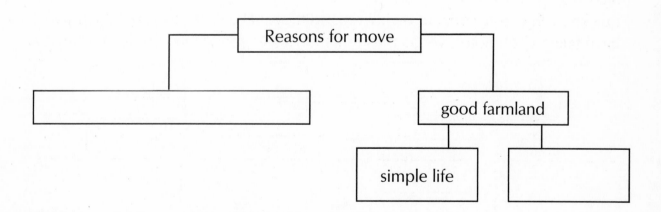

Read more about the customs and lifestyle of the Amish people. Then complete the map.

A lifestyle of simplicity is carried into all aspects of Amish dress and also in Amish homes. Clothing for both men and women is very basic and in few colors. Men wear wide-brimmed black hats and, if they are married, beards. Women and girls wear plain long dresses and bonnets. The women wear no cosmetics or jewelry. Most Amish homes are also plain. They are not adorned with decorative touches like wallpaper, curtains, or pictures on the walls. Since the Amish shun all modern conveniences, there is no electricity in their homes. That means they do not use any form of electrical appliance like radios or televisions. You will probably not find a telephone in an Amish home, either.

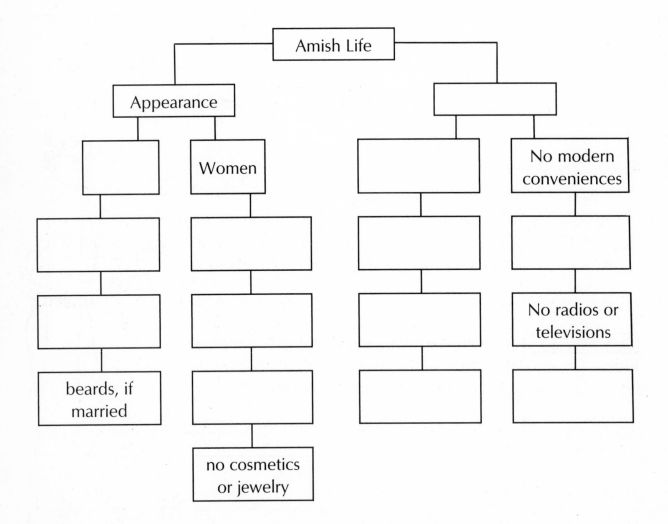

REMEMBER An outline map is a picture of an idea.

Going Fishing

Michael is going to run some errands after he goes fishing. Since he hopes to catch a bass or two, Michael is afraid his excitement may cause him to forget what Mom needs. He has made an outline to help him remember. In this lesson, you will "go fishing" for some important information as you read some interesting facts about fish.

1 KEYS to Outlining

An outline organizes information.

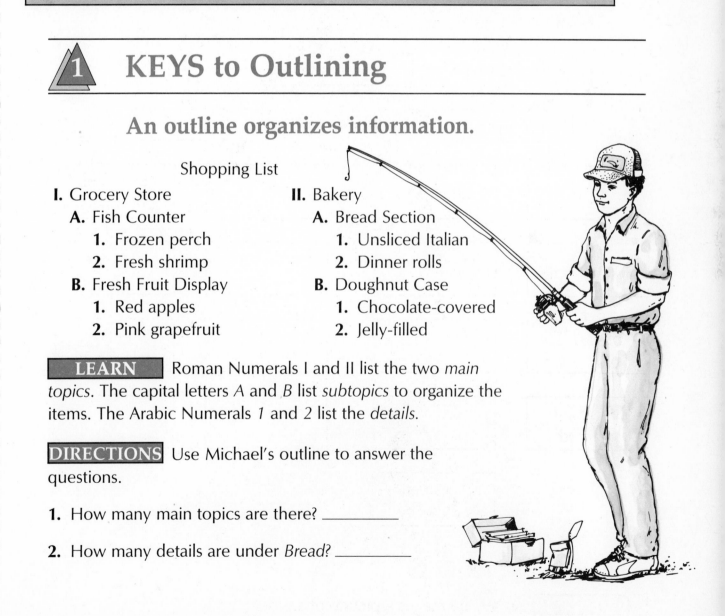

Shopping List

I. Grocery Store
  A. Fish Counter
    1. Frozen perch
    2. Fresh shrimp
  B. Fresh Fruit Display
    1. Red apples
    2. Pink grapefruit

II. Bakery
  A. Bread Section
    1. Unsliced Italian
    2. Dinner rolls
  B. Doughnut Case
    1. Chocolate-covered
    2. Jelly-filled

LEARN Roman Numerals I and II list the two *main topics*. The capital letters *A* and *B* list *subtopics* to organize the items. The Arabic Numerals *1* and *2* list the *details*.

DIRECTIONS Use Michael's outline to answer the questions.

1. How many main topics are there? _____

2. How many details are under *Bread?* _____

Outlining **165**

Read the partial outline. Then answer the questions.

Facts about Sharks

I. Attacks on People

    A. Seldom attack people

        1. Less than thirty per year

        2. Less risky than riding in car

    B. How they attack

        1. Far from shoreline

        2. Swim straight at one person

    C. Why they attack

        1. Sharks eat seals

        2. People look like seals to sharks

1. What is the title of this outline?

_____

_____

2. What is the main topic?

_____

_____

3. Write a subtopic about attacks on people.

_____

_____

_____

4. Write a detail about how sharks attack.

_____

_____

_____

5. Write a detail about why sharks attack.

_____

_____

_____

Read and Apply

DIRECTIONS Look for main topics, subtopics, and details as you read about some unusual kinds of fish. Then read each question and circle the correct answer.

There are many unusual fish. Some are unusual because they eat in a strange way. Other fish are unusual because they look strange.

The Black Swallower eats in a strange way. It has such a large stomach that it can swallow other fish whole and digest them later. The Archer fish is another strange eater. It squirts water at a bug it spots sitting on a leaf. The bug falls into the water from the force of the Archer's squirt. Then the Archer has its dinner.

The Four-eyed fish's name suggests it is a strange-looking fish. A strip of skin across the pupils of its eyes allows it to look above and below the water as it swims along the surface. Kissing fish hold their mouths open and grasp each other by the jaws. They push and pull with their mouths together as if they are kissing.

1. What is this article mainly about?
   a. Where Fish Live
   b. Unusual Fish
   c. Fish That Are Good To Eat

2. What odd thing does the Archer do?
   a. Squirts water
   b. Jumps up and down
   c. Hugs other fish

3. What causes the four-eyed fish to look different?
   a. Stripe on tail
   b. Odd fins
   c. Strip of skin

4. What do kissing fish do to each other?
   a. Ignore
   b. Push and pull
   c. Squirt water

Read each group of words. Tell whether it is a main topic, sub-topic, or detail. Fish out *two* main topics, *four* subtopics, and *eight* details. Some are done for you.

1. Eats fish whole _____

2. Kissing Fish subtopic _____

3. Large stomach _____

4. Four-eyed Fish _____

5. Eat Strangely main topic _____

6. Squirts water at bug _____

7. Strip of skin over pupils _____

8. Archer· _____

9. Grasp by the jaw _____

10. Black Swallower _____

11. Look Strange _____

12. Split-level eyes _____

13. Eats the bug that falls _____

14. Push and pull detail _____

DIRECTIONS Use the phrases above to complete the outline.

I. Eat Strangely _____

   A. _____

      1. _____

      2. _____

   B. _____

      1. _____

      2. _____

II. _____

   A. _____

      1. _____

      2. _____

   B. Kissing Fish _____

      1. Push and pull _____

      2. _____

REMEMBER Subtopics explain main topics, and details explain subtopics.

Marketplaces

Do you think it's fun to go shopping? In this lesson, you'll read about some famous marketplaces in the world as you learn about writing a report.

1 KEYS to Report Writing

A report is written from an outline and organized notes.

LEARN When you write a report, you expand your outline and notes. Main topics in an outline will be the topics of paragraphs in your report. The outline's subtopics and details help you write informative and interesting paragraphs in your own words. You organize your notes by topic and refer to them for help in remembering all the information you read about a subject.

EXAMPLE One or more paragraphs can be written about each of these main topics for a report about world-famous places to shop:

  I. Grand' Place
  II. Piccadilly Circus
  III. The Merchandise Mart
  IV. Stock Market

DIRECTIONS Read each note. Decide which topic the note tells about. Write the topic's Roman Numeral on the line.

_____ **1.** The Mart—covers two city blocks

_____ **2.** Cattle and livestock not sold here

_____ **3.** Sundays—buy birds at Grand' Place

_____ **4.** No clowns or performing animals here

DIRECTIONS Read the notes and outline about a special marketplace. Then complete the paragraphs below as they might be written in a report.

Notes

—In Brussels, Belgium
—Since before 1620 when Pilgrims landed in North America
—Food sold six mornings a week
—Flowers sold in afternoons
—Birds sold on Sundays
—Surrounded by buildings
—Buildings gold-trimmed
—Outdoor market

Marketplaces Outline

I. Grand' Place
  A. In Brussels, Belgium
    1. Outdoor
    2. Gold buildings
    3. Started before 1620
  B. Goods Sold
    1. Food
    2. Flowers
    3. Birds

Grand' Place began long before _____, when the _____ settled in _____. Grand' Place is an _____ marketplace in _____, Belgium. _____ buildings surround Grand' Place.

Many foods are sold in the marketplace from Monday through _____. In the afternoons when all the _____ is sold, the sellers bring out _____. The good smells of _____

and _____ are replaced on Sunday by the singing of _____.

DIRECTIONS Think about what the notes and outline would include as you read about three more interesting marketplaces.

Although Piccadilly Circus bustles with activity, you'll find no clowns or performing animals there. Piccadilly Circus is a round, open area surrounded by fashionable shops in the heart of London. The area takes its name from the word *circus* which means *round and open*. Piccadilly Street is one of six streets coming together at Piccadilly Circus. Besides being the marketplace, the Circle is also the center of London's entertainment center where many theatres, playhouses, and restaurants are located.

In the center of Chicago is another interesting shopping area. The Merchandise Mart is a gigantic building which covers two city blocks. Unlike the shops in Piccadilly Circus, the Merchandise Mart is not open to the public. People who own and operate furniture and home-decorating stores throughout the world shop at the Merchandise Mart. They buy goods to sell in their stores. The Merchandise Mart, which also contains many offices, is the largest commercial building in the world.

The Stock Market, located in New York City, is a marketplace of a different sort. The stock that is bought and sold here is not livestock like cattle and sheep. When people buy and sell stock at the Stock Market on Wall Street, they are buying or selling parts of businesses in the world. The New York Stock Market is one of the largest stock markets in the world.

Read the notes and an outline of the article you just read. Use the notes and outline to write, in your own words, a two-paragraph report about one of the three marketplaces. Write your report on the lines below.

Outline

Piccadilly Circus Notes

– Many shops
– Circle Circus where 6 streets meet
– Theatres, playhouses, restaurants
– In center of London

Stock Market Notes

– In New York City
– Not like cattle and sheep
– On Wall Street
– One of largest in world
– Buy and sell parts of businesses

II. Piccadilly Circus
   A. In London, England
     1. Shopping area
     2. Entertainment center
   B. Name
     1. Circus means circle
     2. Six streets meet

III Stock Market
   A. In New York City
     1. On Wall Street
     2. One of largest in world
   B. Stock
     1. Parts of companies
     2. Not livestock

_____

_____

_____

_____

_____

_____

_____

_____

REMEMBER Notes and an outline are guides to writing a report.

Testing, 1 ... 2 ... 3 ...

A test shows whether something works or is understood. In this lesson, you'll learn some information that will help you take different kinds of tests.

△ 1 KEYS to Test–Taking

Test questions may be asked in different ways.

LEARN A *pre*test is taken to see how much you know about a subject *before* you study it. A *post*test is taken *after* you study. There are different ways that you can be asked to tell what you know. Pretests and posttests may use one or several of the following:

TYPE OF QUESTION	WHAT YOU DO
Multiple choice	Choose from several answers.
True-False	Mark a statement true or false.
Matching	Find items that go together.
Sentence completion	Fill in a missing word or words.
Essay	Discuss something in your own written words.

DIRECTIONS Circle *T* if the statement is true. Circle *F* if the statement is false.

1. A posttest and a pretest are the same thing. T   F

2. More than one kind of question may be on a test. T   F

3. If you draw a line from a word to its definition, the question is a matching question. T   F

4. If you're asked to write what you think of taking tests, the question is a multiple-choice question. T   F

② Practice Test–Taking

DIRECTIONS Read each question. Write the name of the type of question on the line. Then write or circle the answer.

_____ 1. A spelling test given on a Monday is usually

called a _____ .

_____ 2. Before taking a posttest, you will want to

    a. stretch your leg muscles.

    b. review the subject matter to be tested.

    c. read the next week's chapter.

    d. read every book in your classroom.

_____ 3. Tell which type of test question you like best

and why you prefer it. _____

_____

_____

_____ 4. After you have learned how to multiply by 5,

you might be given a _____

over problems such as _4 times 5._

_____ 5. A posttest comes before a pretest.   T   F

_____ 6. Match the term with its definition by writing
the correct letter on the line.

    _____ essay   **a.** an item on a test

    _____ test   **b.** a type of test question

    _____ question   **c.** to read and review

    _____ study   **d.** checks for understanding

DIRECTIONS Read the story to learn more test-taking tips.

"Angie, wait!" called Teri, as she ran to catch up with her friend. "What did you think of the social studies test?"

"I think I did pretty well, except for a few true-false questions and one multiple-choice question about inventors," replied Angie. "Those true-false questions were hard, didn't you think?"

"Well, actually, I thought they were easy. I just looked for those key words we learned about. Did you remember that a question must be *totally* true to be marked true? Mr. Seely said that words like *always, never, only,* and *usually* need to be read carefully when deciding whether a statement is true or false, and one of those words was in nearly every question! That sure helped me!" said Teri.

"I forgot part of what Mr. Seely said, but I did read each question very carefully," sighed Angie. "I hope I didn't mess up. How did you answer that multiple-choice question about the inventors?"

"The men were all inventors, so I marked *all of the above.* I'm sure it was right," answered Teri.

"Whew, so did I! Did you have any trouble with the matching questions?" Angie asked her friend.

"I was almost confused when I noticed that some of the words could be matched to more than one of the choices. I marked both answers when that happened. Sure hope that's what I was supposed to do."

Angie stopped suddenly, "So did I! Do you suppose he was checking to see if we were awake?"

"And were you?" came a deep voice from behind.

Teri and Angie turned abruptly in surprise, upon hearing Mr. Seely's voice. "I . . . I think so!" they chimed in unison.

"I've only glanced at your test papers, but it looked like you both remembered all those tips we talked about in class. Did you have any problem with the essay question?" their teacher asked.

Angie responded quickly, "Oh, no! It was like writing a story about some of my favorite inventors."

"How about you, Teri? Did you remember to include an opinion now and then and to draw a conclusion about how the inventions have affected your life today?" asked Mr. Seely.

"I *think* I did all of that," said Teri, hopefully.

"We'll see, ladies. I'm going off to grade the tests now. You think *taking* a test is tough, I'll bet, but look! You each had *one* test and *I* have to grade all twenty-four!"

"There's an easy solution to that problem, Mr. Seely!" Angie called to Mr. Seely who, for some reason, pretended not to hear.

DIRECTIONS Use information from the story to answer the questions.

1. What four words can be helpful in deciding if a statement is true or false?

   _____

   _____

   _____

   _____

2. What should you look for if several choices are correct in a multiple-choice question?

   _____

   _____

   _____

   _____

3. What might be included in an answer to an essay question?

   _____

   _____

   _____

   _____

4. What do you need to look for in matching questions?

   _____

   _____

   _____

   _____

REMEMBER Test-taking skills are helpful in taking tests.

3: How to Catch a Snake Alive

Anansi went away. He heard all the animals laughing at him from every corner of the jungle.

This meeting had happened on a Monday morning, and Anansi went home and sat down to think of a plan. At last he hit upon an idea. He would build a vine trap for Snake.

So on Tuesday morning he built a vine trap. He found a strong vine and made a noose with it. Inside the noose, he put some of Snake's favorite berries. Then he hid the vine in the grass and waited.

On hearing these words, all the animals in the jungle laughed. The frogs laughed, the parrots laughed, but Tiger laughed loudest of all.

How could a weak, stupid animal like Anansi catch Snake alive and bring him to Tiger?

After a short while, Snake came long the path. He saw the berries and went towards them. He slithered across the vine and ate the berries. Anansi pulled at the vine to tighten the noose, but Snake's body was too heavy and the noose could not hold him. Anansi saw that his vine trap had failed.

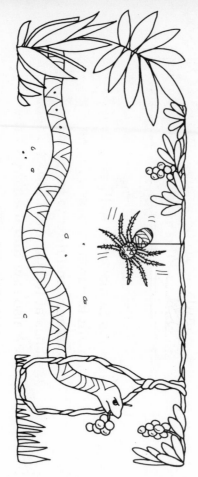

The next day was Wednesday and Anansi tried another plan. He dug a deep hole in the ground and made the sides slippery with grease. At the bottom of the hole he put some bananas. Snake loved bananas. Then Anansi hid in the bushes and waited.

"What is it you want me to do?" asked Anansi eagerly.

"It is only a small thing," said Tiger. "Do you know Snake, who lives down by the river? I want you to bring me Snake alive, Anansi. If you bring me Snake alive, you can have the stories named after you."

Tiger stopped speaking. He did not move his tail. He looked at Anansi and waited for him to speak. All the animals in the jungle waited for Anansi to speak: the frogs in the water and the parrots in the trees. All watched Anansi, waiting to laugh at him.

At last Anansi spoke. "Tiger, I will do as you ask."

Soon Snake came slithering along the path towards the river, for he was hungry and thirsty. He saw the bananas at the bottom of the hole, but he also saw that the sides of the hole were slippery.

So he wrapped his tail around the trunk of a tree and then reached down into the hole and ate the bananas. When he had finished, he pulled himself up with his tail and slithered away.

Anansi had lost his bananas and he had lost Snake, too.

Thursday morning came and Anansi made a fly-up trap. Inside the trap he put an egg. Again Snake came along the path towards the river. When he saw the egg, he lifted his head and a third of his body up from the ground. Then he carefully lowered his head into the trap and picked up the egg in his mouth. He didn't even touch the trap, so the fly-up trap didn't catch Snake either.

Tiger moved his tail very slowly from side to side and said, "Very well, Anansi, I will let the stories be named after you if you do something for me."

"Yes, yes!" replied Anansi. "I will do anything that you ask."

"Yes, I'm sure you will," said Tiger, moving his tail slowly from side to side.

Friday morning came and Anansi didn't know what to do. He sat and thought all day. Saturday morning came and still Anansi didn't know how he could catch Snake alive.

Anansi went for a walk down to the river. He came to the hole where Snake lived and there was Snake. His body was hidden in the hole but his head was resting on the ground at the entrance to the hole. It was early morning and Snake was watching the sunrise above the mountains.

Now Tiger liked all these stories very much, and he was very proud that they were named after him. He wanted them to be called "Tiger Stories" forever.

He thought to himself, "How stupid and weak Anansi is. I will play a trick on him so all the animals can laugh at him."

"Good morning, Anansi," said Snake.

"Good morning, Snake," said Anansi.

"Anansi, I am very angry with you," said Snake. "You have been trying to catch me all this week. You set a fly-up trap to catch me. The day before that you made a slippery hole for me. And the day before that you made a vine trap. I have a good mind to kill you, Anansi!"

"Ah, you are too clever, Snake," said Anansi. "You are much too clever for me."

"Everyone knows that I am the weakest of us all," Anansi went on, "and that is why I have nothing named after me. Tiger, would you let something be named after me so that people may know my name too?"

"And what would you like to have named after you?" asked Tiger, without even looking at Anansi.

"The stories!" cried Anansi. "The Tiger Stories! The stories that every-one tells in the jungle in the evening at sunset. The stories about Br'er Snake and Br'er Cow and Br'er Bird and all the rest of us."

4: The Final Plan

Anansi and Snake went on talking.

"What you say is true," said Anansi. "I did try to catch you all this week, but I failed. Now I can never prove that you are the longest animal in the world, longer even than the bamboo tree."

"Of course I am the longest of all the animals," cried Snake. "And I am much longer than a bamboo tree."

"What! Longer than that bamboo tree over there?" asked Anansi.

"Of course I am," said Snake. "Look and see."

Anansi bowed low. He bowed so low that his head touched the ground. Tiger did not say hello to him, but just looked at him.

"Good morning, Tiger," said Anansi. "I have a favor to ask of you."

"What is it?" asked Tiger.

"We all know that you, Tiger, are the strongest of us all," said Anansi. "That is why you have so many things named after you. Tiger lilies, tiger stories, tiger moths, tiger snakes, tiger sharks, tiger this and tiger that!"

Snake came out of his hole and stretched himself out full length.

"Yes, you are very, very long," said Anansi, "but the bamboo tree is very long too. Now that I look at you and at the bamboo tree, I must say that the bamboo tree looks longer. But it is hard to tell, because it is further away."

"Well, bring it nearer," cried Snake. "Cut it down and put it down beside me. You will soon see that I am much longer than the bamboo tree."

So Anansi ran to the bamboo tree and cut it down. He placed it on the ground and cut off all its branches.

"Now, put it down beside me," said Snake.

Anansi put the long bamboo tree on the ground beside Snake.

2: The Meeting

One day, not long after that, Tiger and Anansi, the strongest and the weakest animals, met face to face. They met in a clearing in the forest.

Frogs and toads hiding in the cool water watched them. Green parrots perched high in the trees watched them.

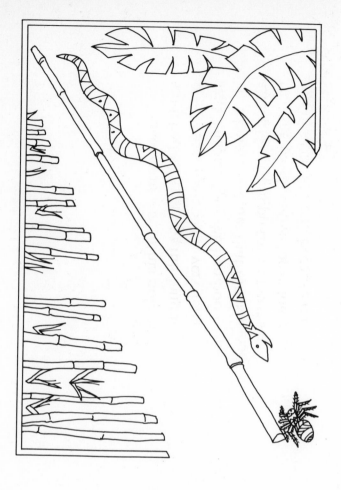

Sometimes they would talk about which animal was the strongest.

"Who is the strongest of us all?" asked the snake.

"The tiger is the strongest of us all," cried the frog. "When Tiger whispers everyone listens, even the trees. When Tiger is angry and roars loudly, the trees tremble."

"And who is the weakest of us all?" asked the snake.

"Anansi!" shouted the frog.

"Anansi, the spider, is the weakest of us all."

All the animals laughed.

When Anansi whispers, nobody listens. When Anansi shouts out, everybody laughs. So all the animals sat in a circle, laughing about Anansi.

Then Anansi said, "Snake, when I go up to see where your head is, you will sneak up. When I go down to see where your tail is, you will sneak down. In that way you will always seem to be longer than the bamboo tree, which is really longer than you are."

"Tie my tail to the end of the bamboo tree then," cried Snake. "Tie my tail! I know that I am longer than the bamboo tree, whatever you say."

So Anansi tied Snake's tail to the end of the bamboo tree and then ran up to the other end.

"Stretch, Snake, stretch! We shall see if you are longer."

By this time a crowd of animals had gathered around. This was better than a race.

"Stretch, Snake, stretch!" they shouted.

Snake stretched as hard as he could. Anansi tied him round his middle to the bamboo tree so he would not slip back.

"Stretch, Snake, stretch!" they shouted.

"Now, one more time, stretch!" cried Anansi.

Snake knew that if he stretched hard enough he could be as long as the bamboo tree.

1: The King of the Forest

Once upon a time, long, long ago, the tiger was king of the forest. At the end of every day all the animals would meet and sit in a circle. They would laugh and talk together and sometimes they would tell stories to each other. These stories were always called the "Tiger Stories."

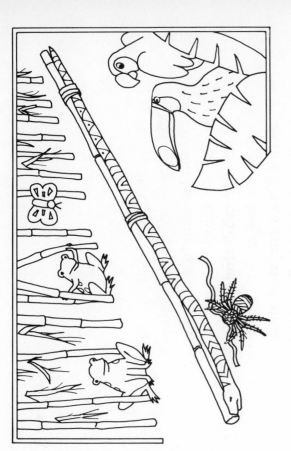

Anansi ran up to him.

"Have a rest for a minute, Snake, and then stretch again. If you can stretch another ten centimeters, then you will be longer than the bamboo tree. Try your hardest. Shut your eyes and stretch. Ready?"

"Yes," said Snake.

Then Snake made a mighty effort. He shut his eyes tightly and stretched and stretched.

"Come on! Come on!" cried the animals. "Just four centimeters more!"

At that moment Anansi ran and tied Snake's head to the bamboo tree. At last he had caught Snake alive!

All the animals fell silent. There was Snake, all tied up and ready to be taken to Tiger. And it was the weak and stupid Anansi who had caught Snake all by himself. They could not laugh at him any more.

Never again did Tiger dare call the stories by his name. From that day on, the stories were always known as the "Anansi Stories."

Contents

23

From Tiger to Anansi